Waterdown Ontario in Colour Photos, Saving Our History One Photo at a Time

Photography
by Barbara Raué
2014

Series Name:
Cruising Ontario

Book 60: Waterdown in Colour

Cover photo: 299 Dundas Street

Series Name: Cruising Ontario
Saving Our History One Photo at a Time

Photos in full colour
Check the Appendixes in the back of each book for
descriptions of architectural terms and building styles

Other Books by Barbara Raue

Coins of Gold

Arrows, Indians and Love

The Life and Times of Barbara
Volume 1: Inventions That Have Enhanced My Life
Volume 2: Entertainment That I Have Enjoyed
Volume 3: East Coast Trips
Volume 4: Olympics Have Always Intrigued Me
Volume 5: Wonders of the World
Volume 6: Caribbean Cruises We Have Enjoyed
Volume 7: Animals
Volume 8: Storms and Other Major Disasters in My Lifetime
Volume 9: Wars, Terrorist Attacks and Major Disasters

The Cromwell Family Book

Waterdown

Waterdown is located east of the junction of Highways 5 and 6, the intersection known as Clappison's Corners.

Established in 1792, the Township of Flamborough was named after a prominent geographical formation, the Flamborough Head, and the Town of Flamborough in East Yorkshire, England. The most striking aspect of Flamborough Head are the white chalk cliffs that surround it. The chalk lies in distinct horizontal layers with a layer of glacial deposits at the top of the cliffs

Alexander Brown of the North West Fur Company purchased 800 acres and built a log cabin and sawmill at the top of the Great Falls in present-day Smokey Hollow in 1805. He was the first European settler in the region and was a key figure in the community throughout his lifetime. He moved down Grindstone Creek to the site of present-day LaSalle Park and built "Brown's Wharf". Smokey Hollow was the site of saw, grist, and flour mills, a woollen mill, a brass foundry, tanneries, rake, cradle, and basket factories. Brown built the first school of the village in 1815 on the site of the present-day American House, and employed Mary Hopkins as its first teacher. Entrepreneur Ebenezer Culver Griffin arrived in 1823, purchased more than half of Alexander Brown's property, and had his property surveyed in village lots, the true beginning of the Village of Waterdown.

In 1854, Flamborough was divided into two separate townships, East and West Flaborough. Included within East Flamborough was the town of Waterdown, named because of its close proximity to the place where Grindstone Creek tumbles over the Niagara Escarpment. Mills were built along the creek with the water harnessed to provide power.

Table of Contents

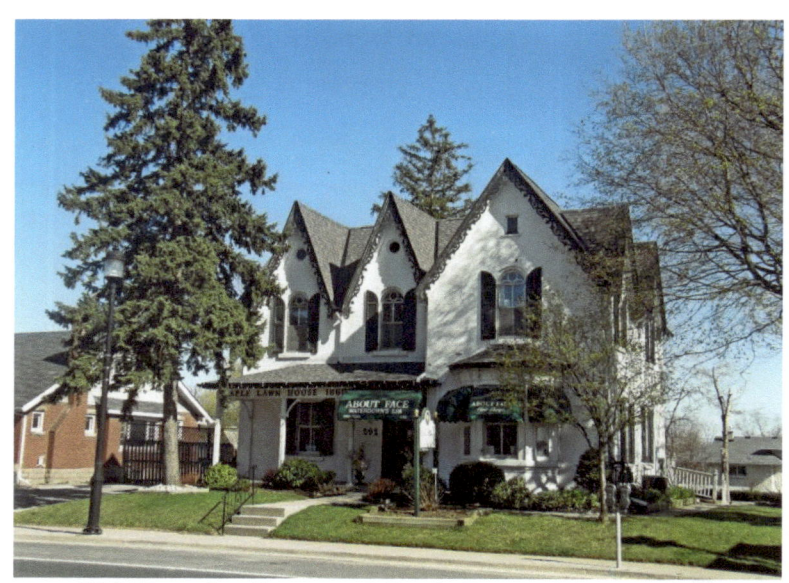

292 Dundas Street – Maple Lawn House 1860
Gothic Revival, Vergeboard trim on gables

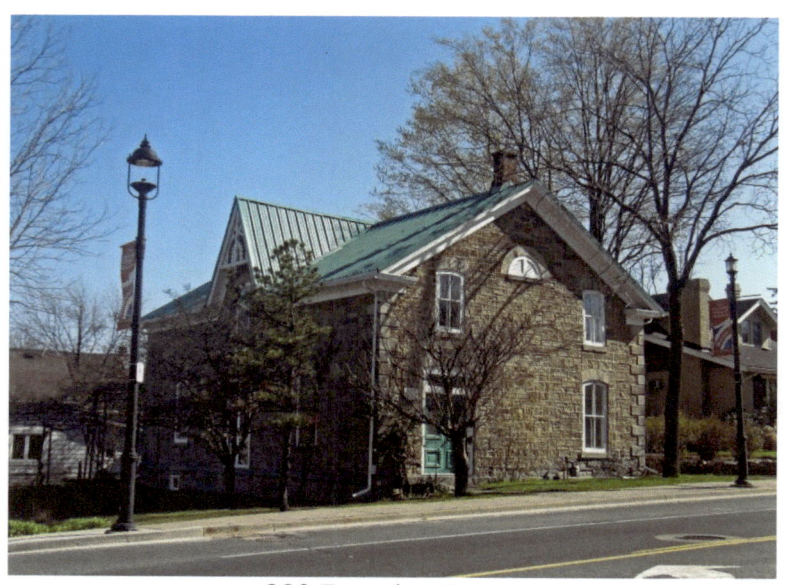

298 Dundas Street

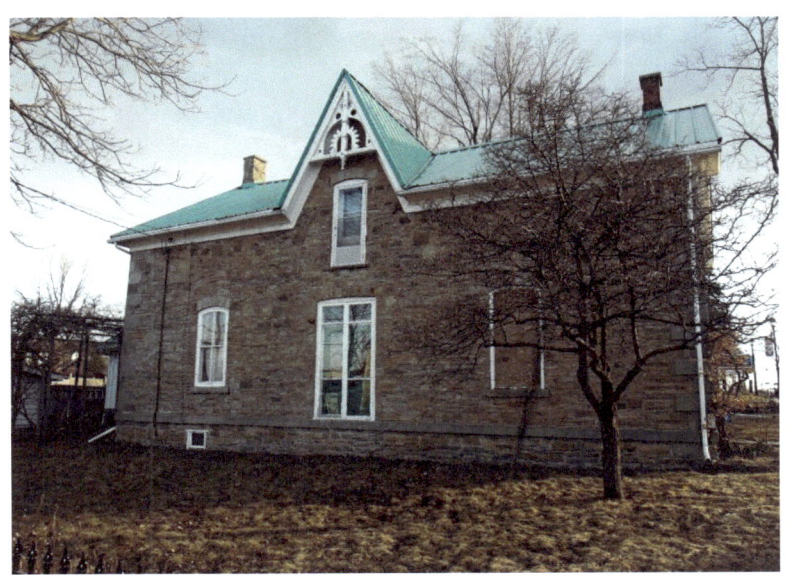

298 Dundas Street – The Old New Connection 1859
Gothic Revival, stone building

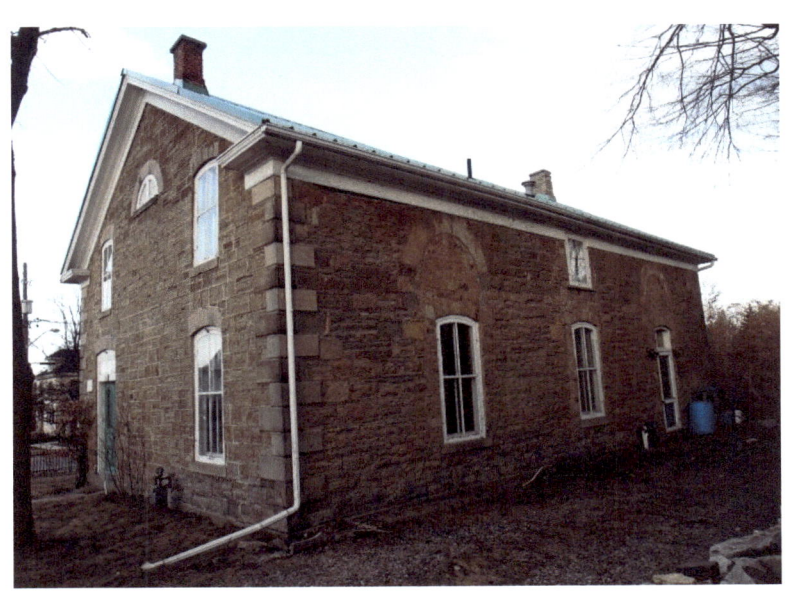

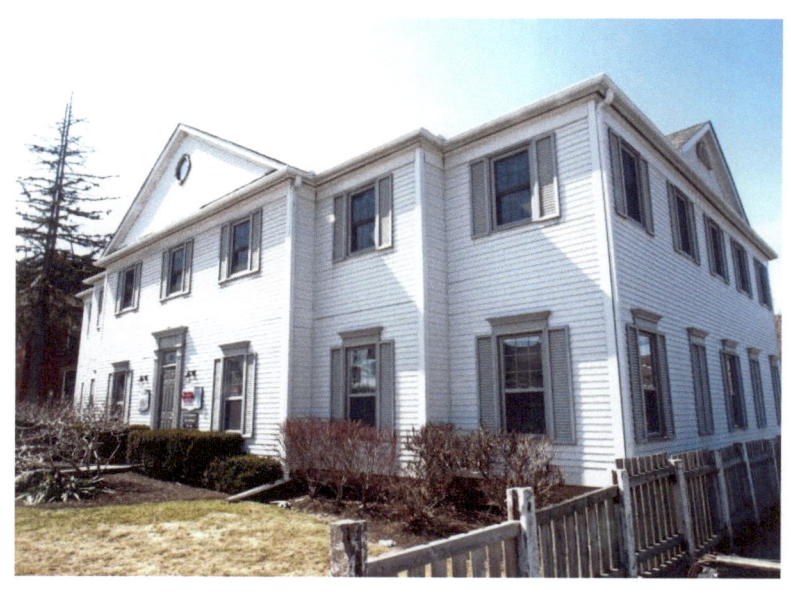

301 Dundas Street – Italianate style

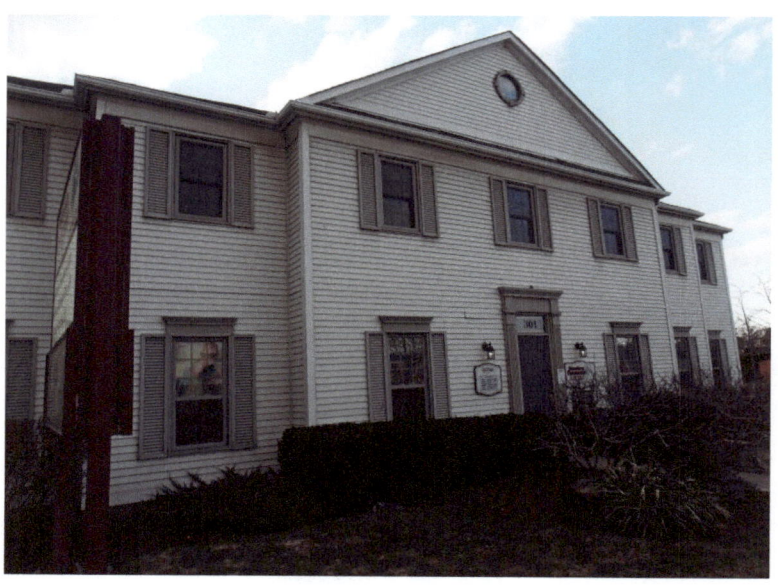

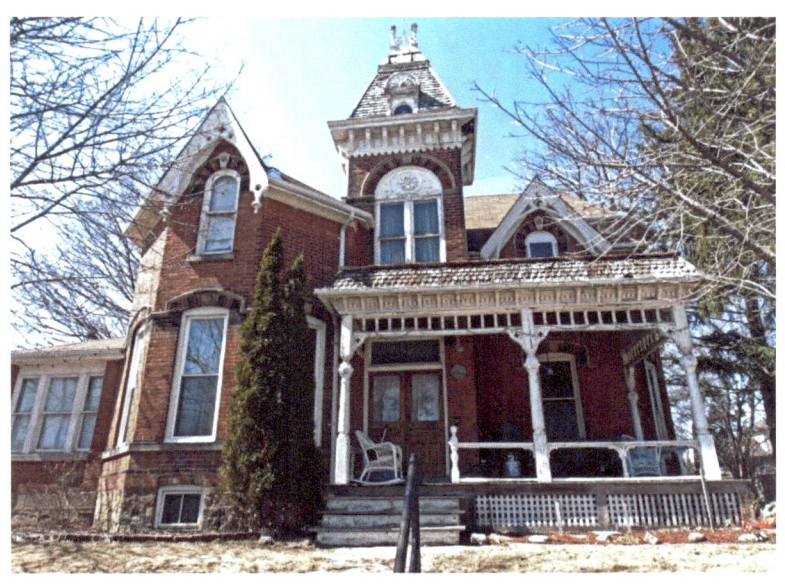

289 Dundas Street – Queen Anne style

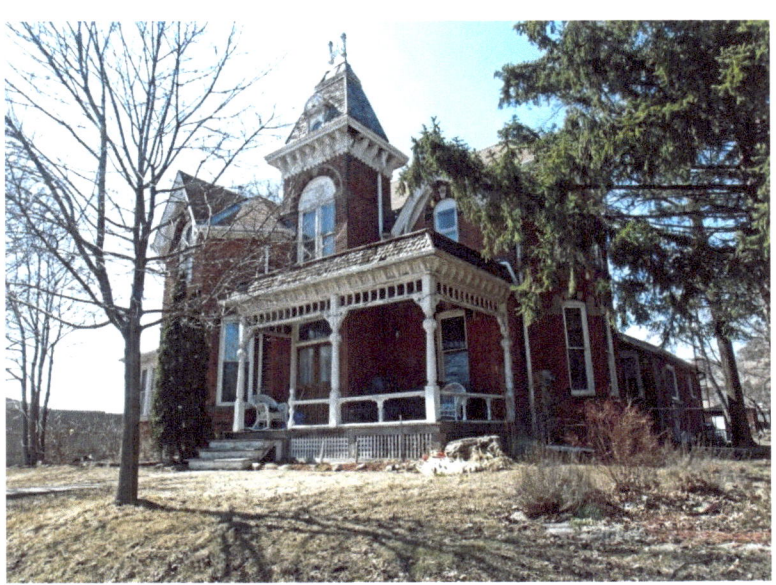

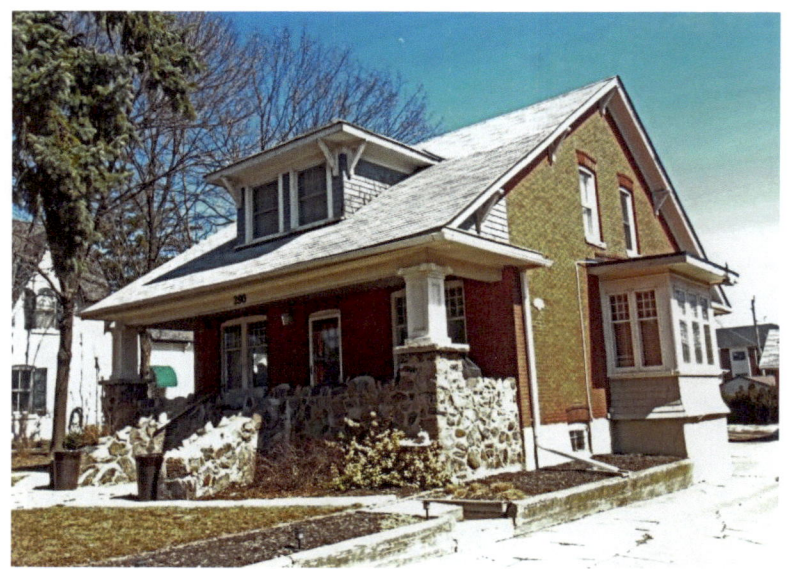

290 Dundas Street – Gothic Revival, dormer in attic

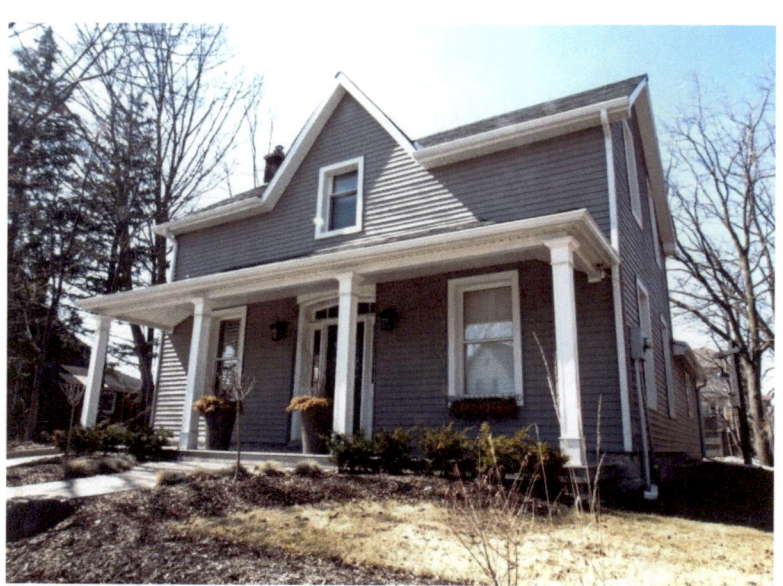

291 Dundas Street – Gothic Revival

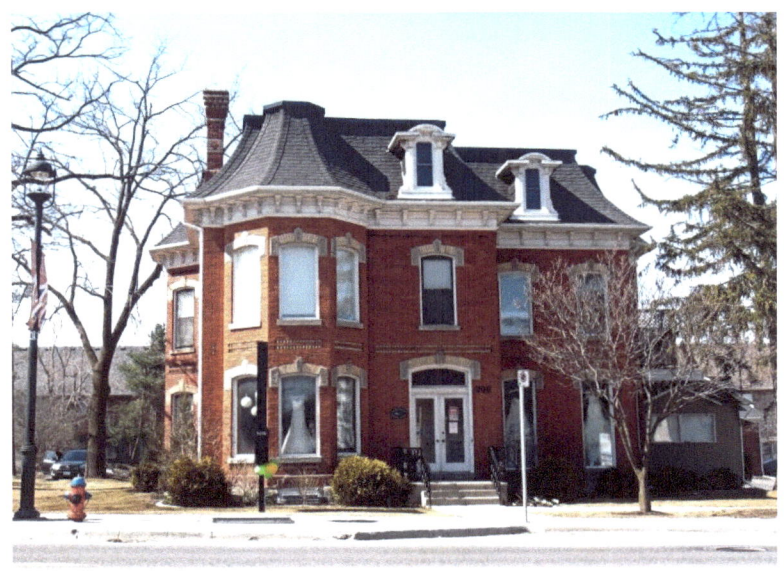

299 Dundas Street – Second Empire style, mansard roof, dormers in roof, cornice brackets, two-storey tower-like bays

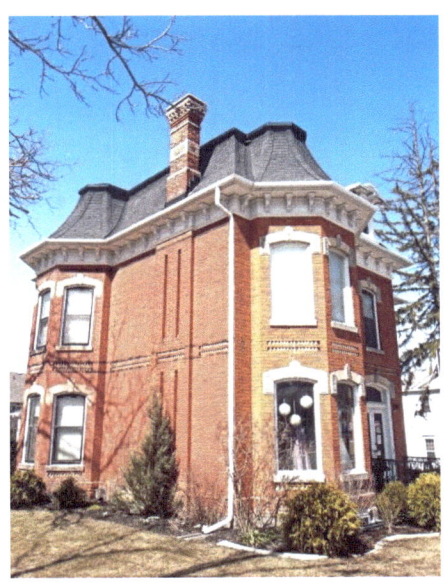

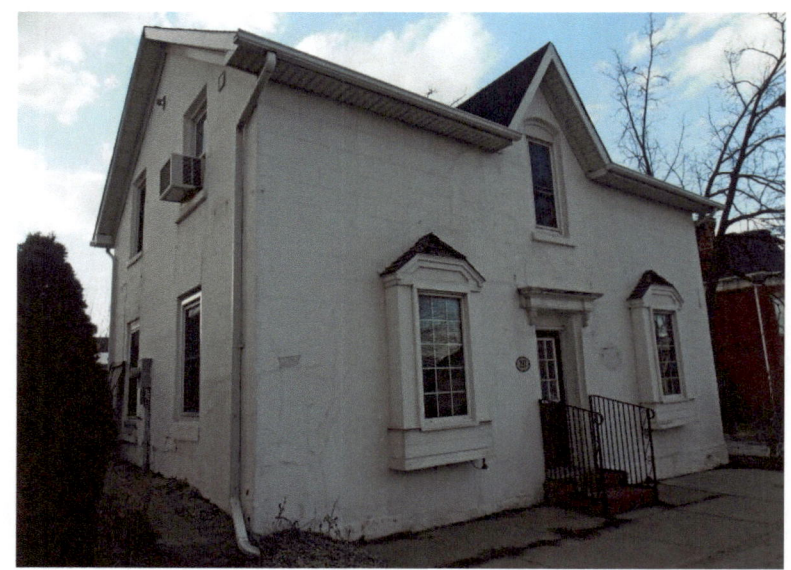

297 Dundas Street – Gothic Revival

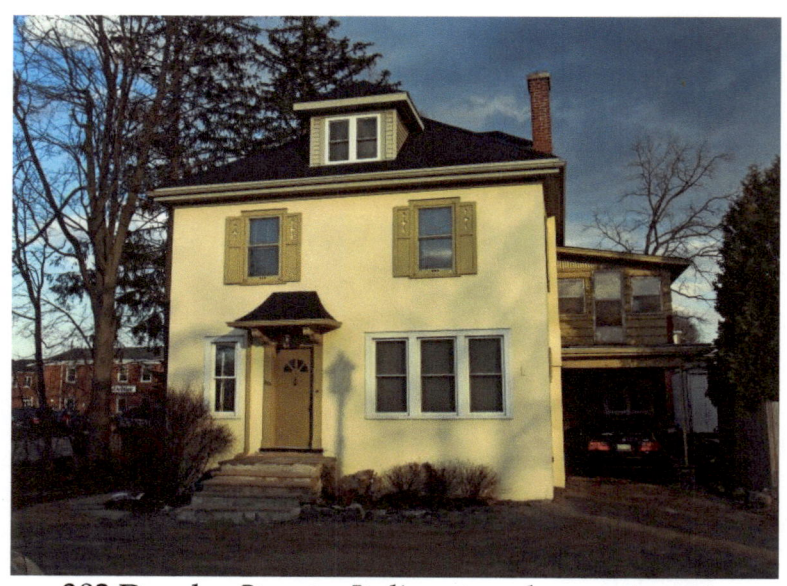

302 Dundas Street – Italianate – dormer in attic

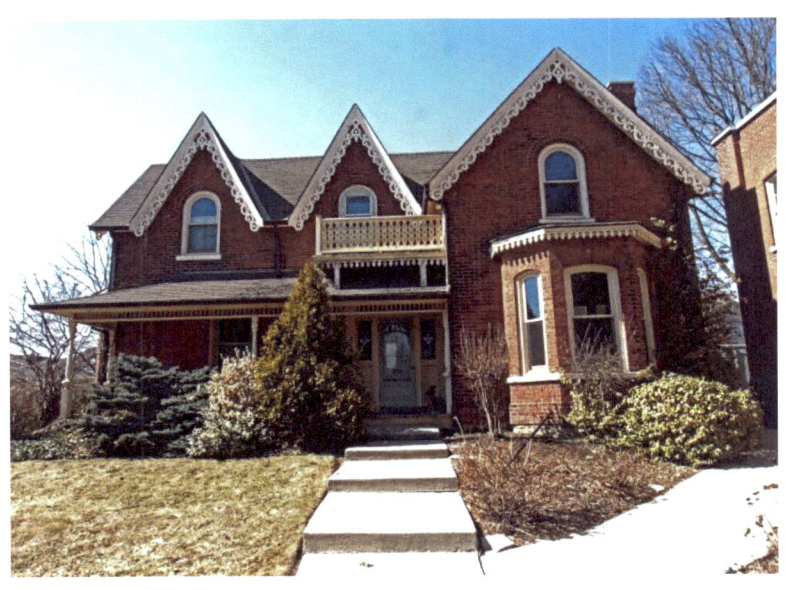

315 Dundas Street East – "Chestnut Grove" - Gothic Revival,
Vergeboard trim, first floor bay windows, built in 1880,
second storey verandah

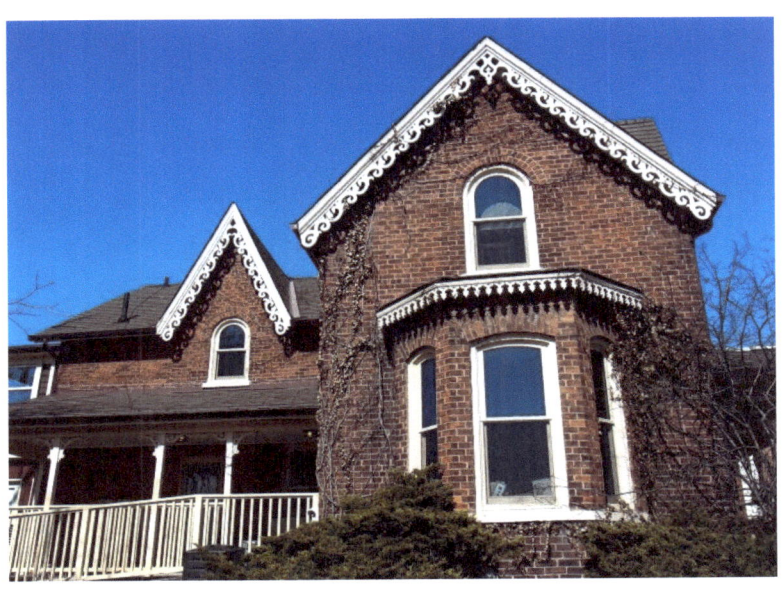

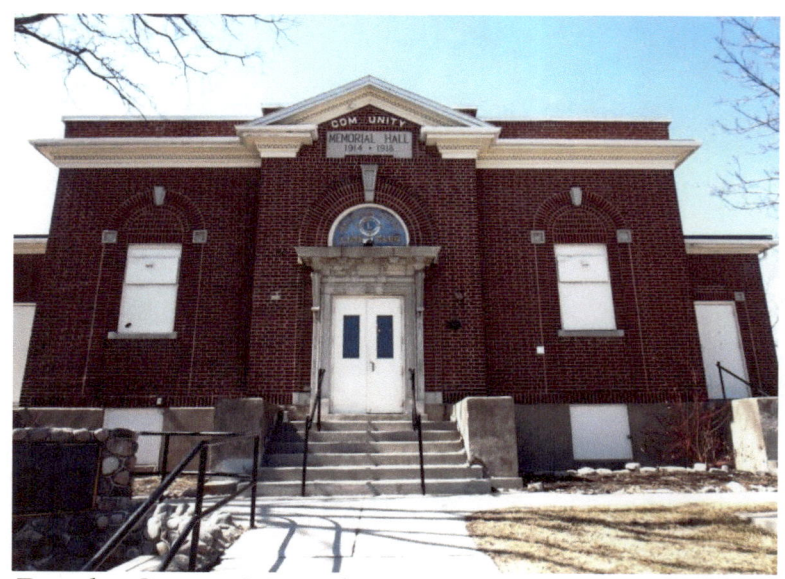

Dundas Street - Waterdown Memorial Hall 1914-1918

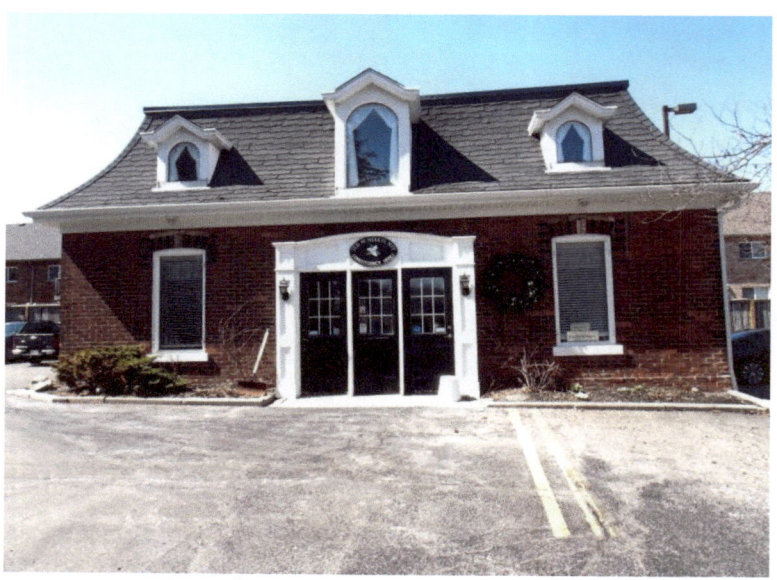

Dundas Street – dormers in roof

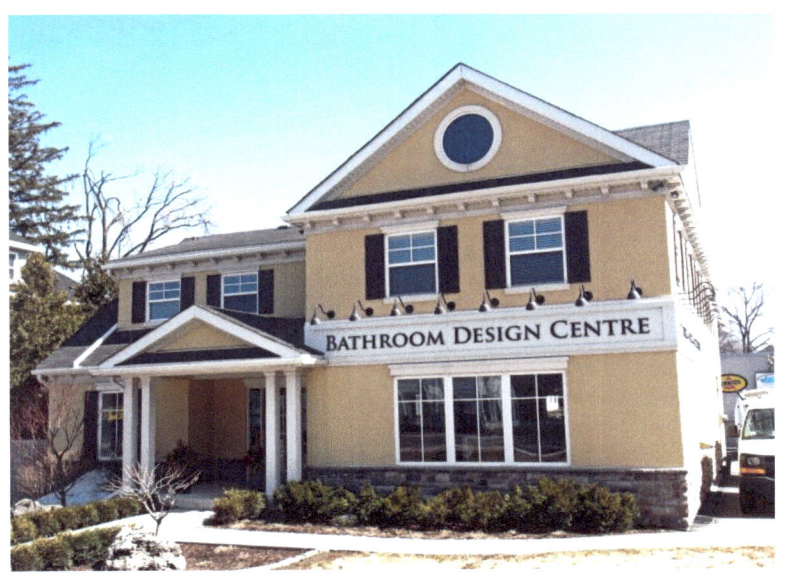

Dundas Street

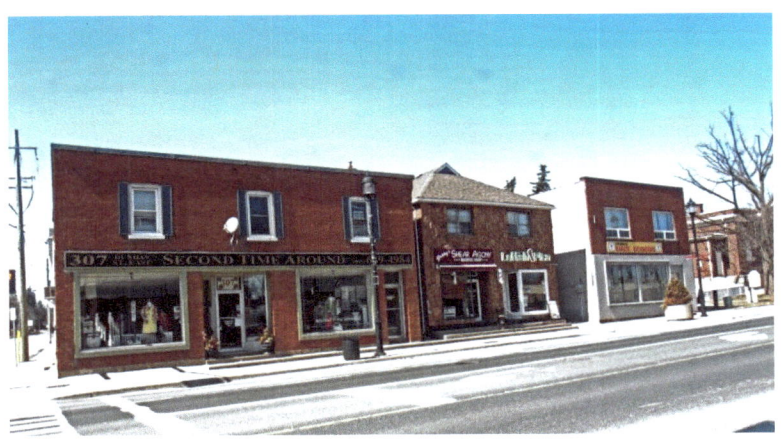

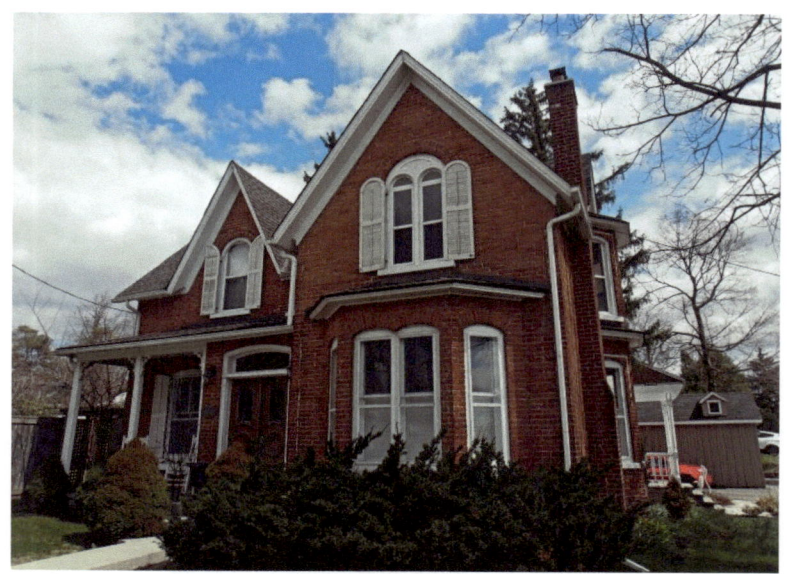

344 Dundas Street – Gothic Revival, bay window on ground floor

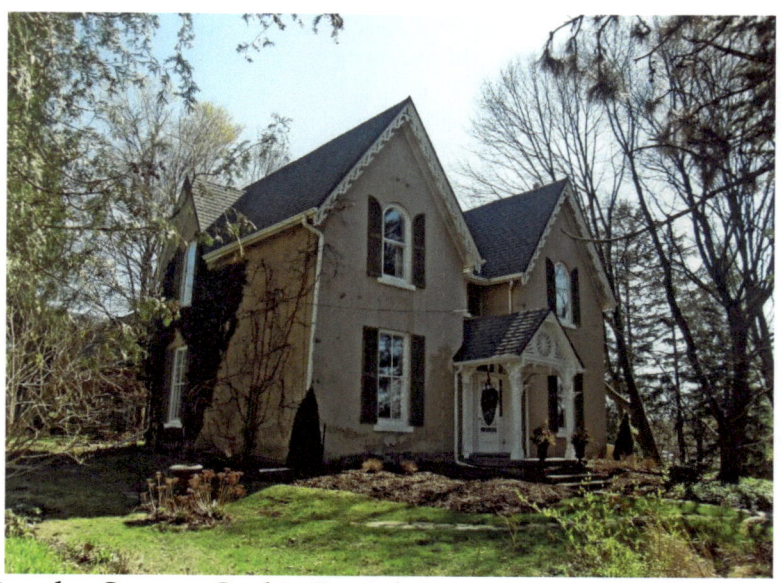

Dundas Street - Gothic Revial, Vergeboard trim on gables

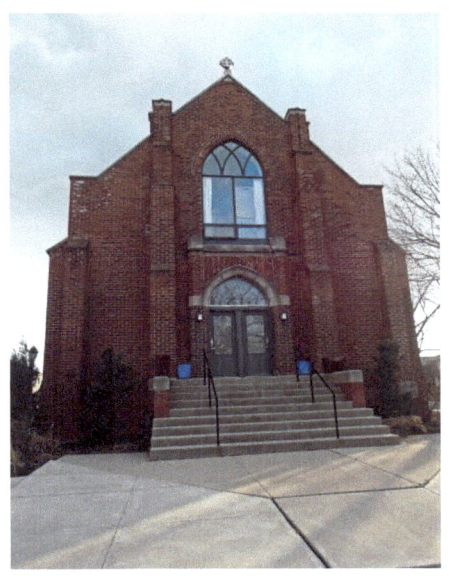

Flamboro Street – former St. Thomas Catholic Paris Church,
A.D. 1914 - now condominiums

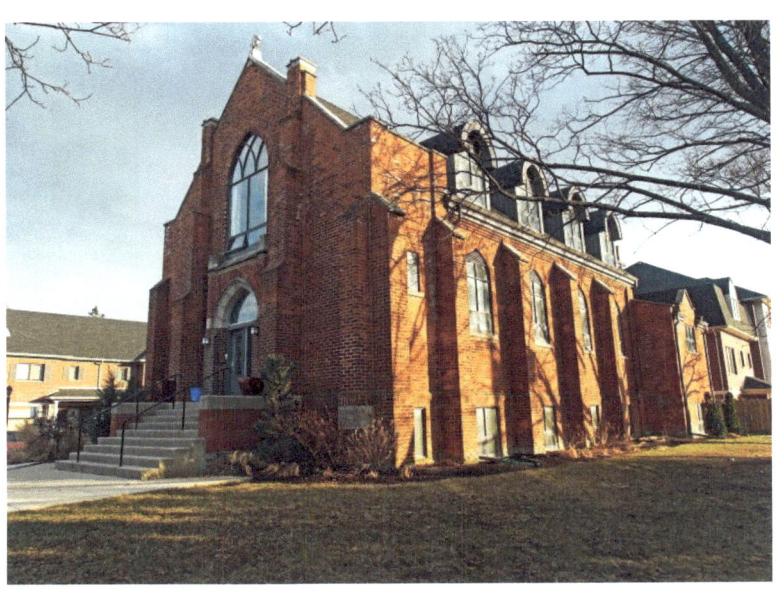

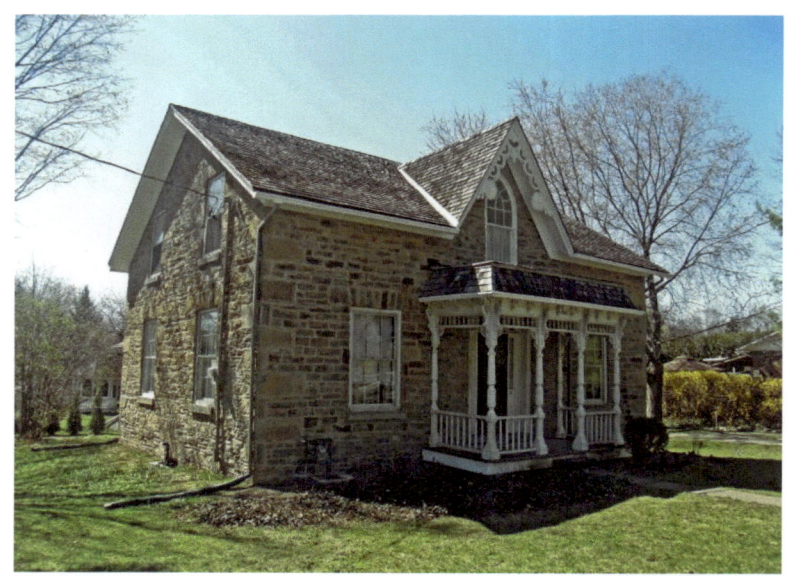

134 Mill Street – Gothic Revival – cobblestone architecture, Vergeboard trim

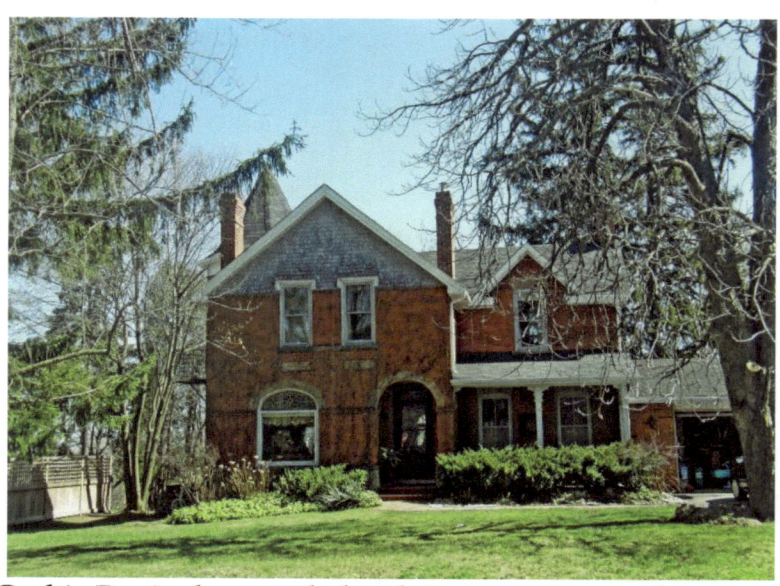

Gothic Revival, turret behind, Romanesque style curved window hoods

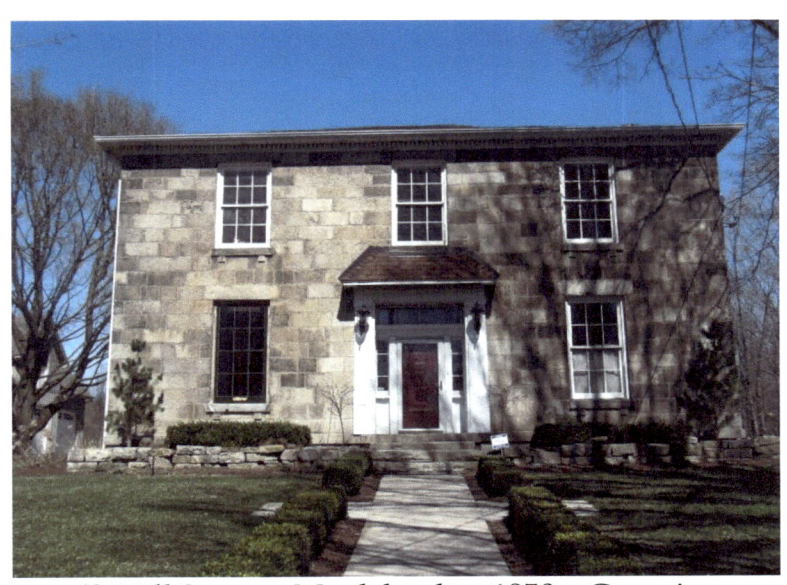

63 Mill Street – Maplebank c. 1850 – Georgian

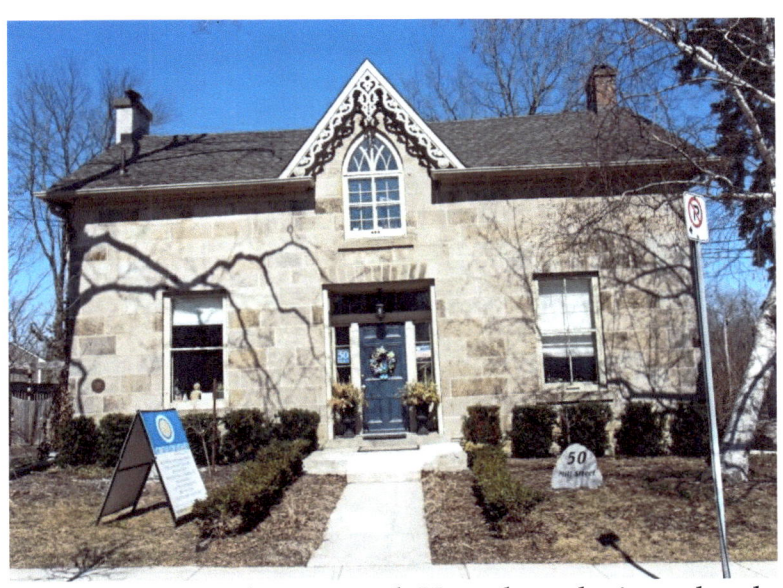

50 Mill Street – Gothic Revival, Vergeboard trim, – local cut stone façade, large ornate Gothic window in centre gable c. 1865

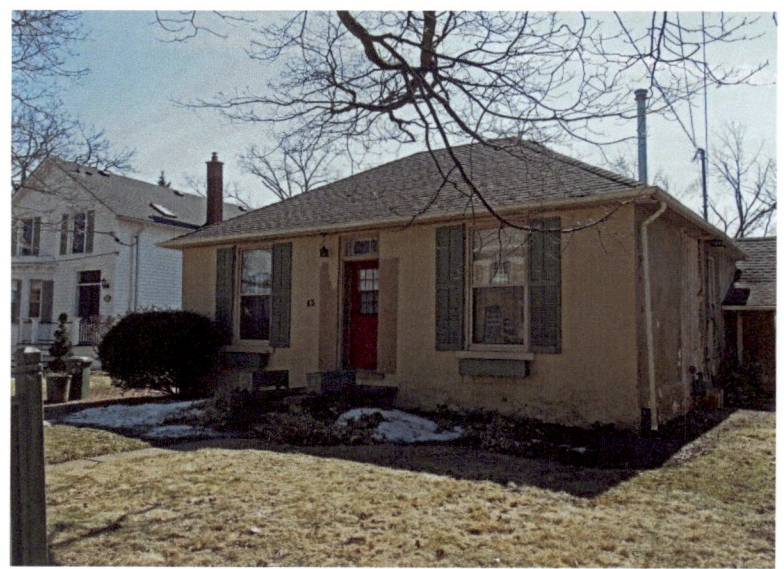

43 Mill Street – Regency Cottage – c. 1850s

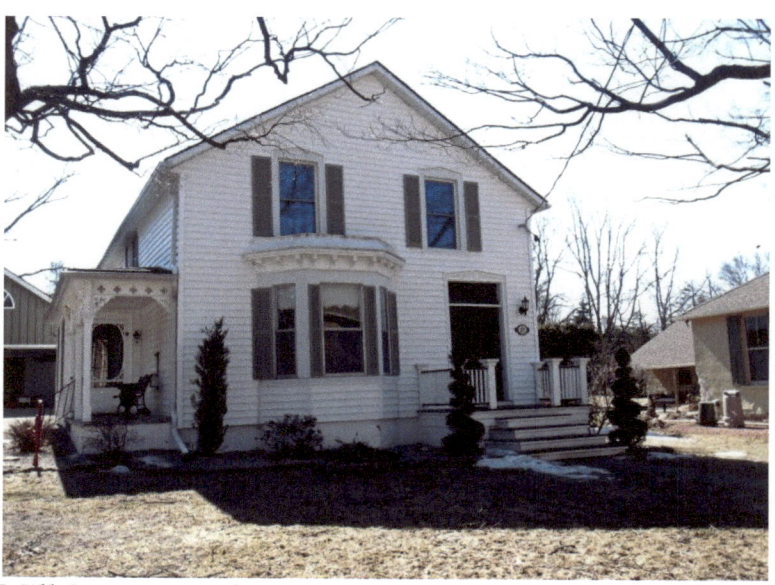

37 Mill Street – Gothic Revival, bay window on ground floor

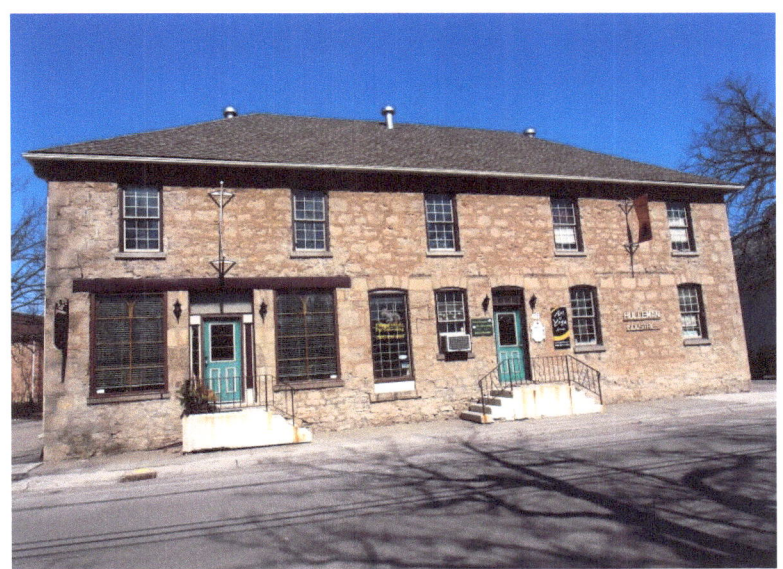

40-42 Mill Street – Georgian – c. 1850s

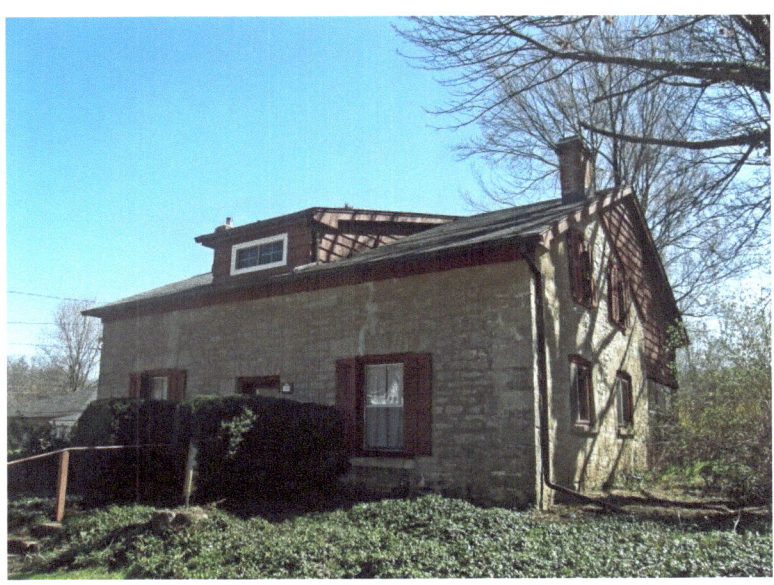

36 Mill Street – The Eastwood Place - Gothic – dormer in roof

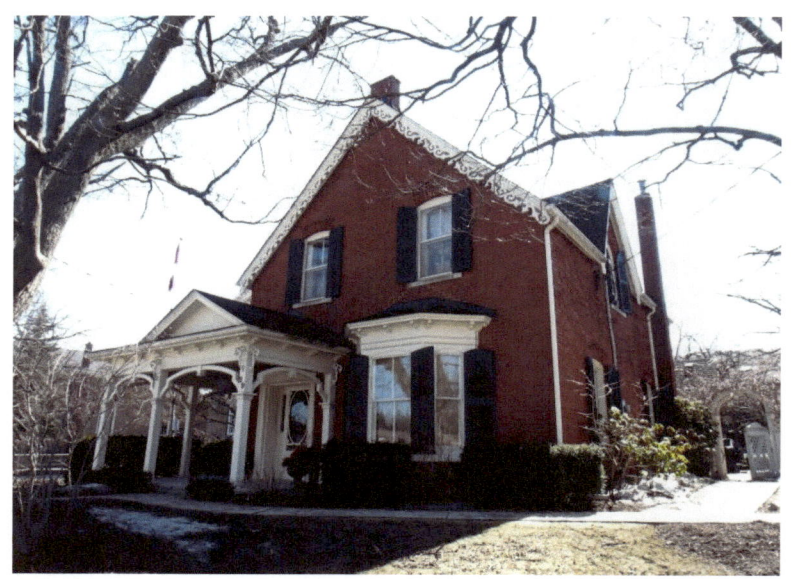

29 Mill Street – Gothic Revival – Vergeboard trim on gable

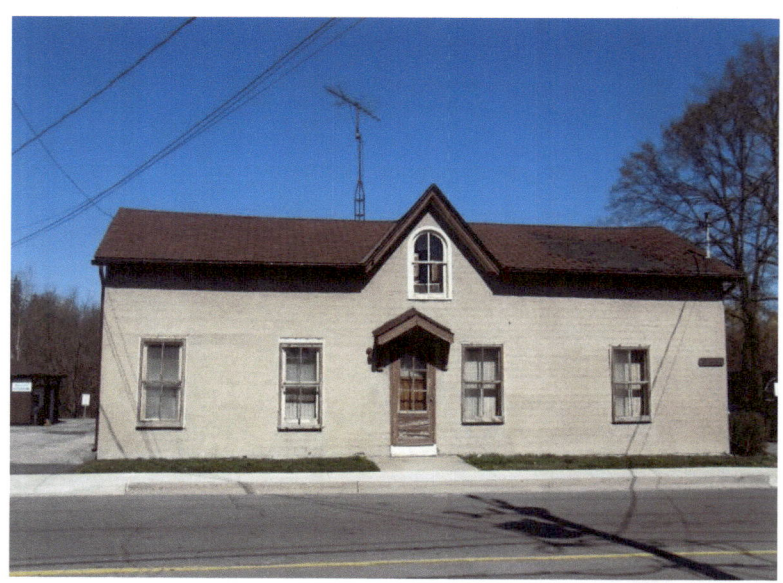

19 Mill Street – Gothic Revival cottage

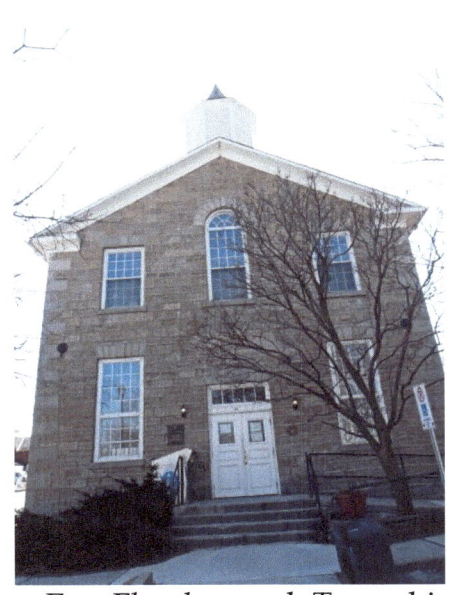

25 Mill Street – East Flamborough Township Hall built of locally quarried limestone

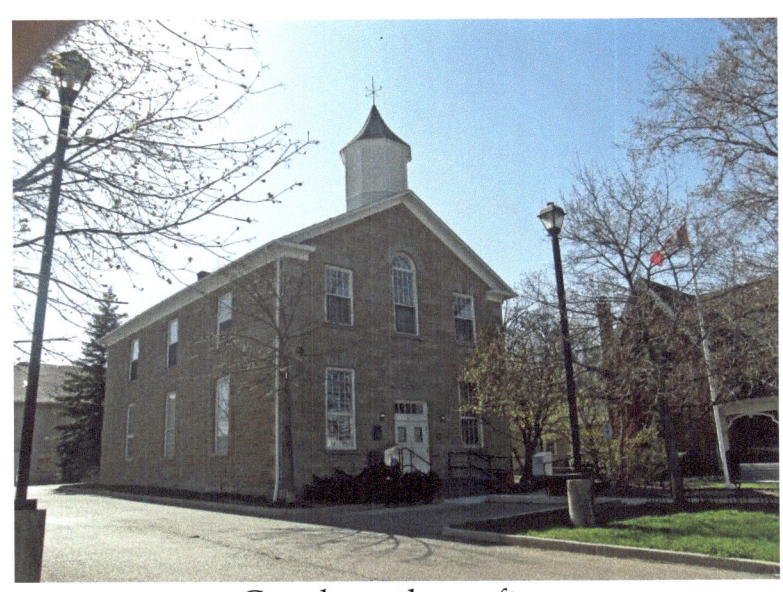

Cupola on the rooftop

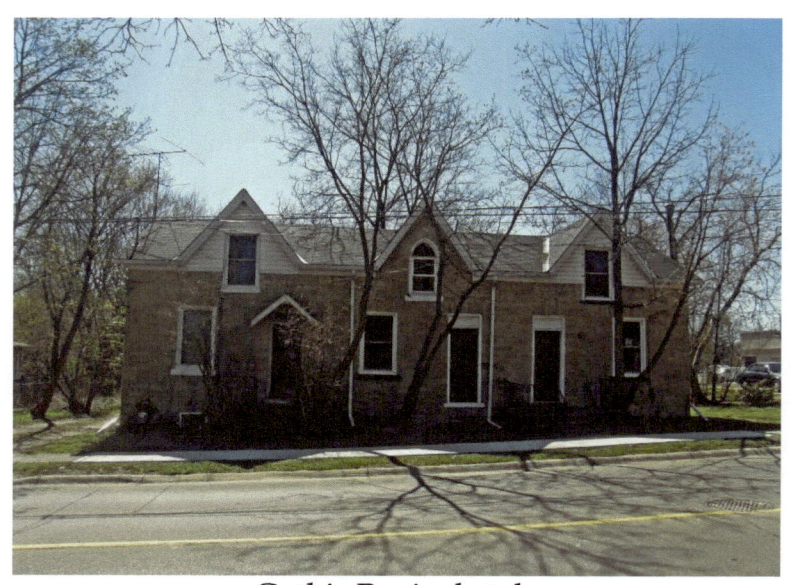

Gothic Revival style

Mill Street

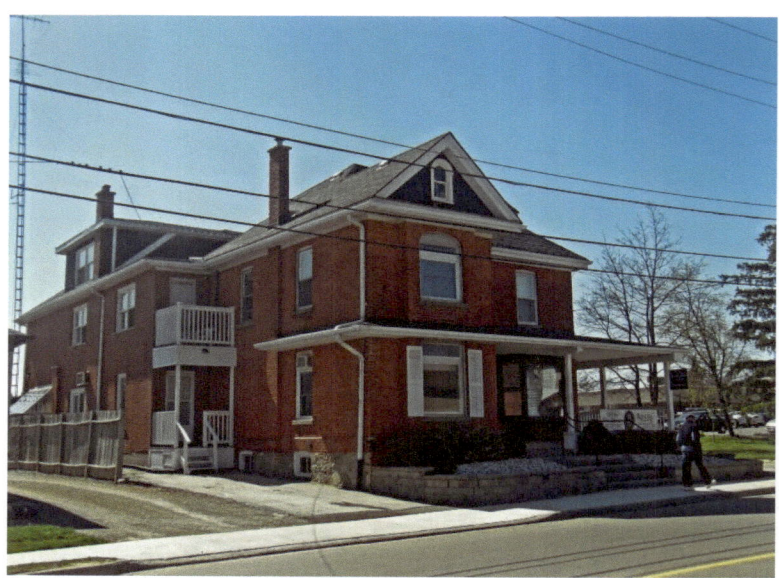

Edwardian style

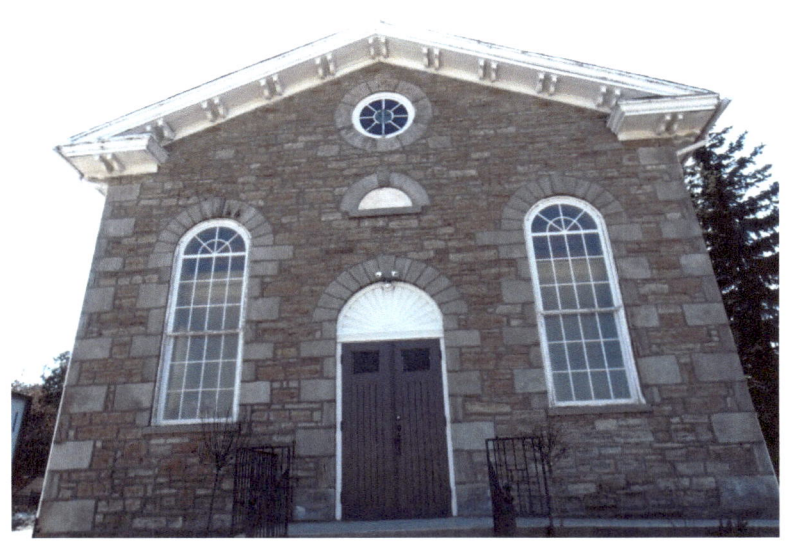

Mill Street – Wesleyan Methodist Church – c. 1838, covered in stone in 1865 - Gothic Revival, cobblestone architecture, cornice return on gable, brackets

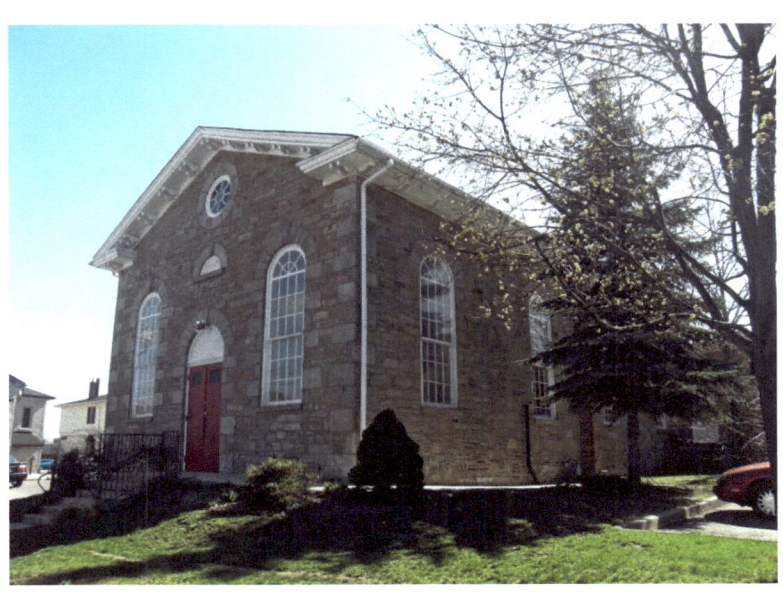

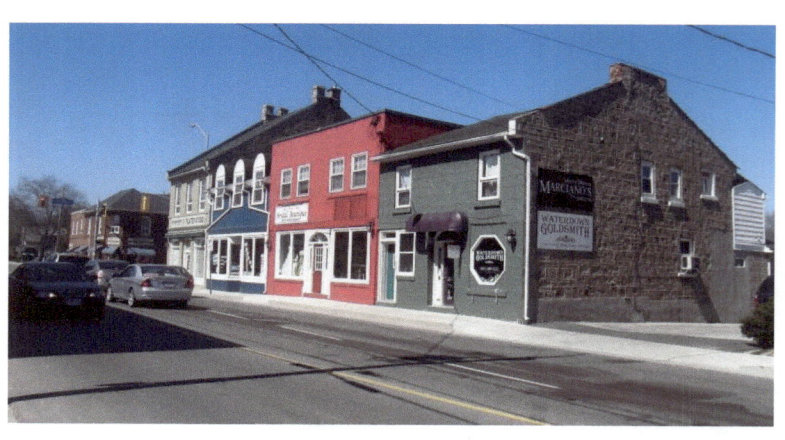

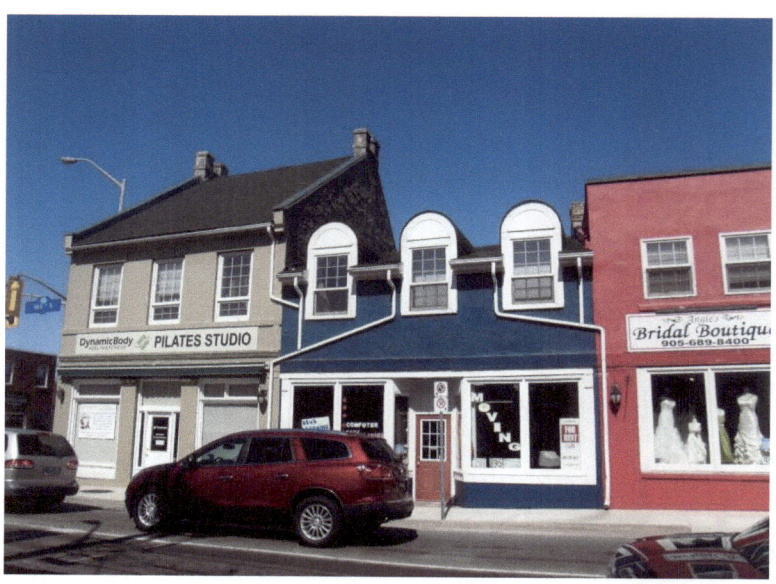

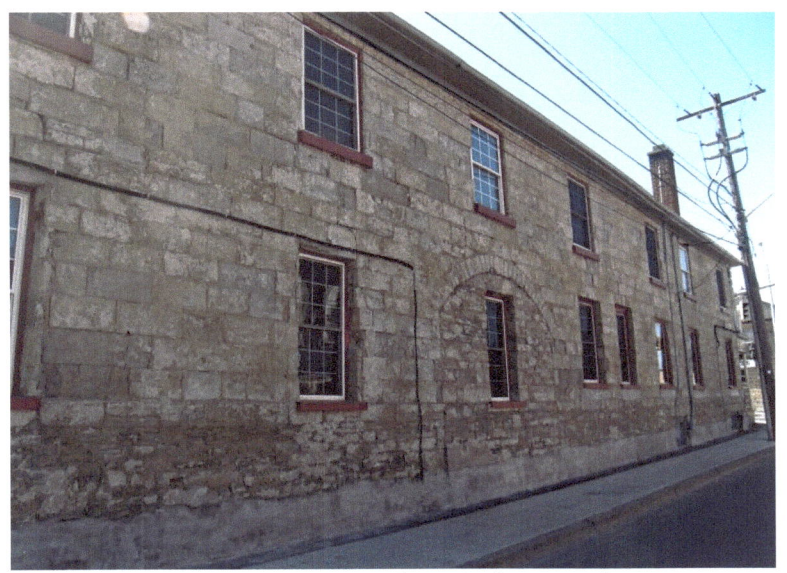

Romanesque style window arch

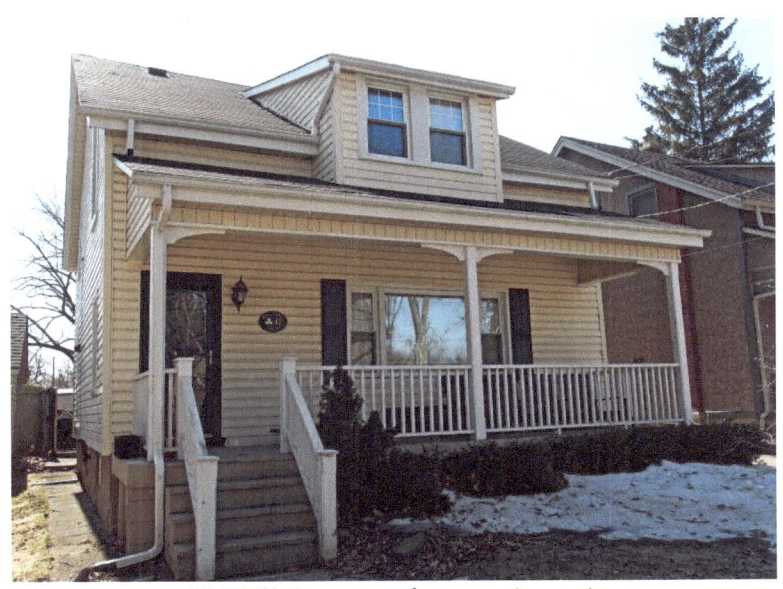

47 Mill Street – dormer in attic

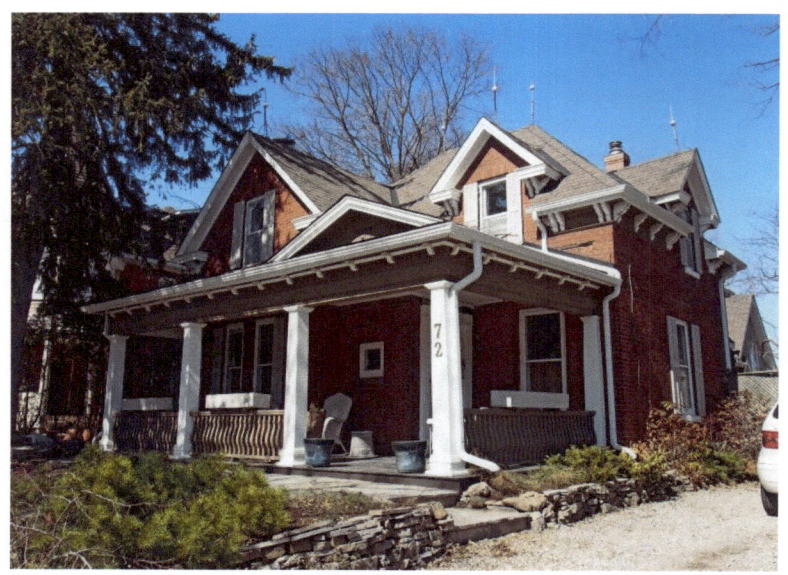

72 Mill Street – Gothic Revival, cornice brackets

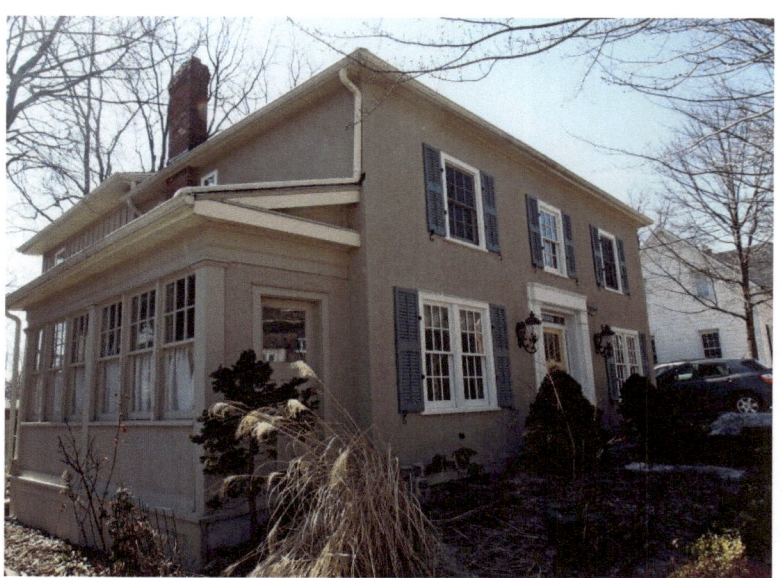

Walnut Shade c. 1852 - Georgian

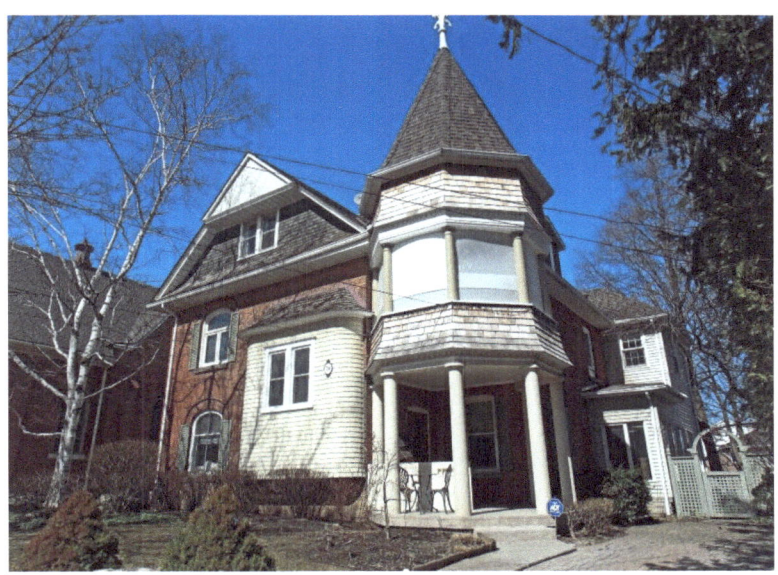

76 Mill Street – the Old Slater House – c. 1890 - Queen Anne style, two-storey octagonal tower, round Doric columns

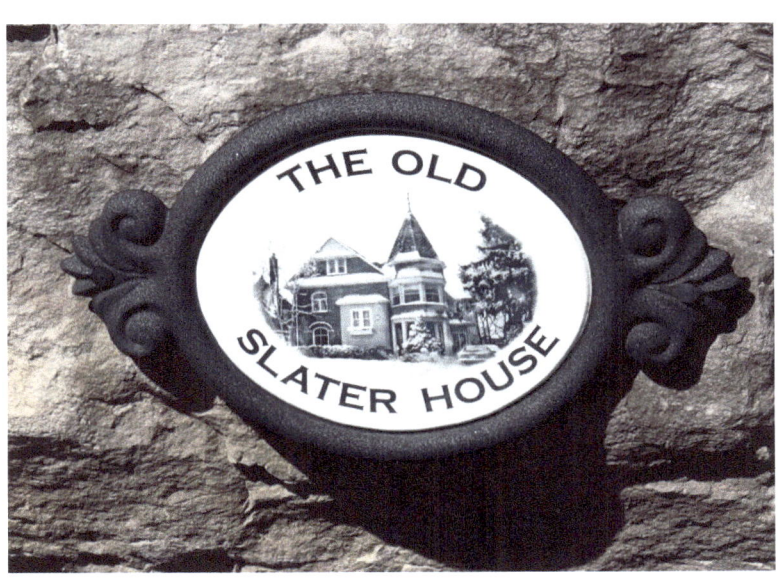

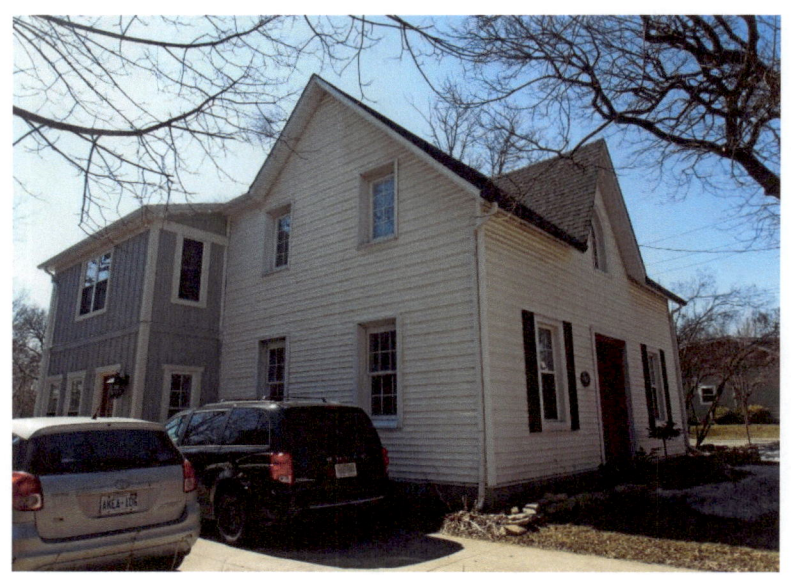

81 Mill Street – Gothic Revival

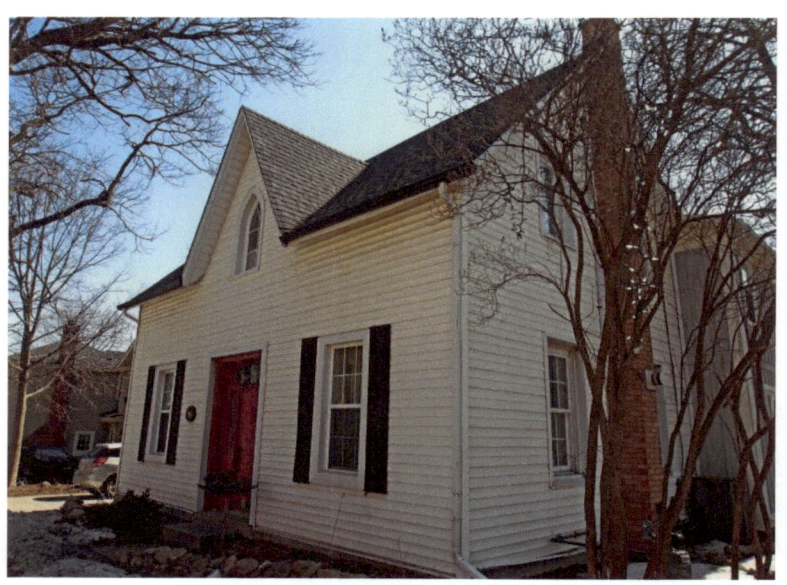

93 Mill Street – Gothic Revival

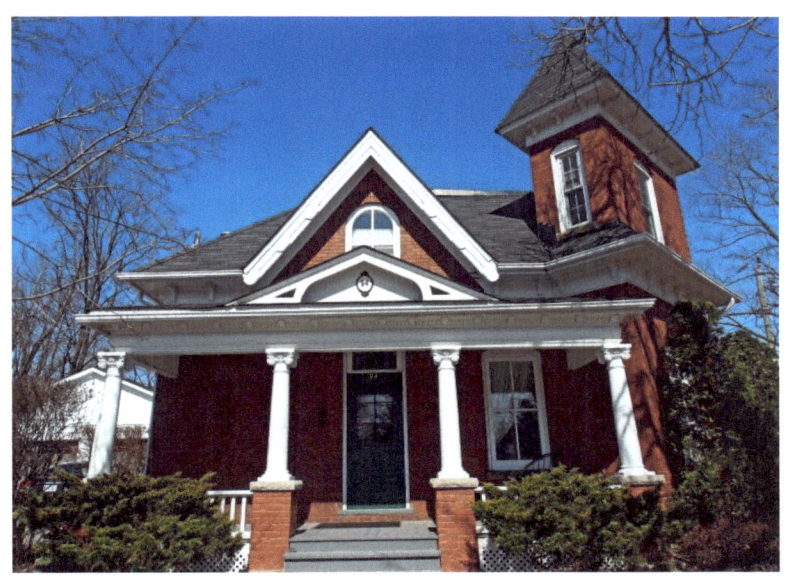

94 Mill Street – Queen Anne style – turret, pediment

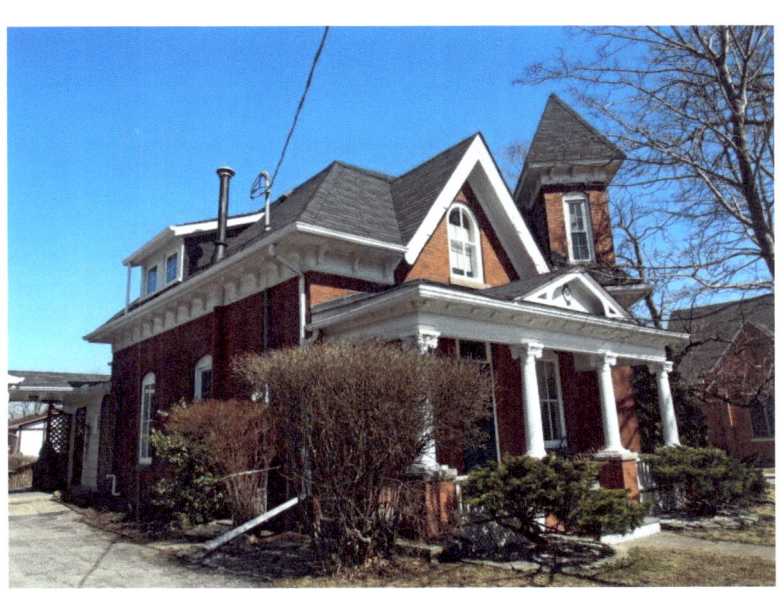

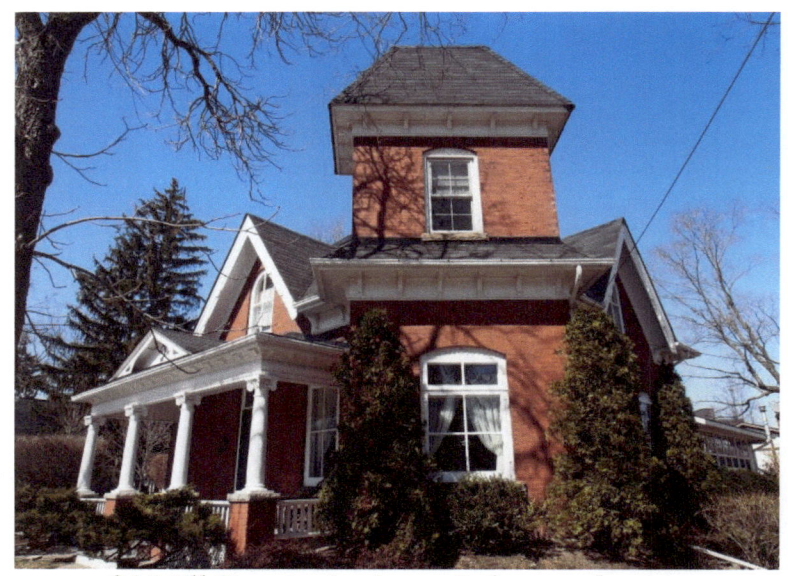

94 Mill Street – ionic capitals on columns

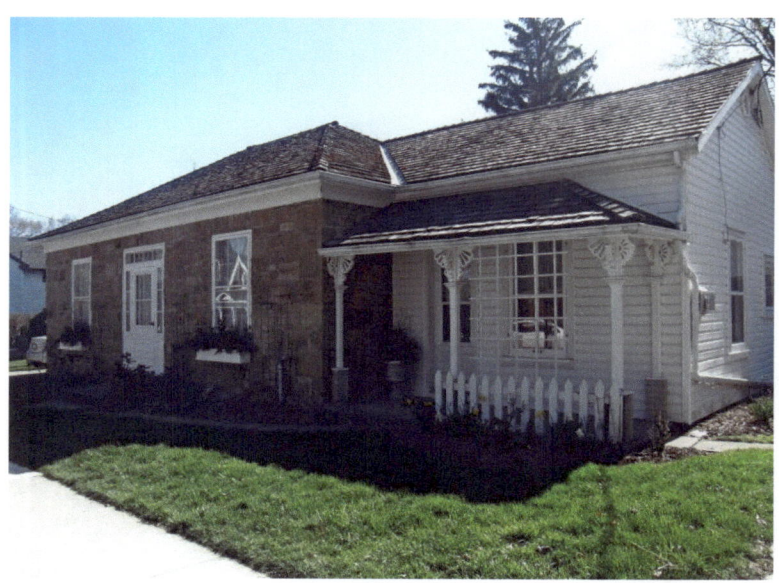

107 Mill Street

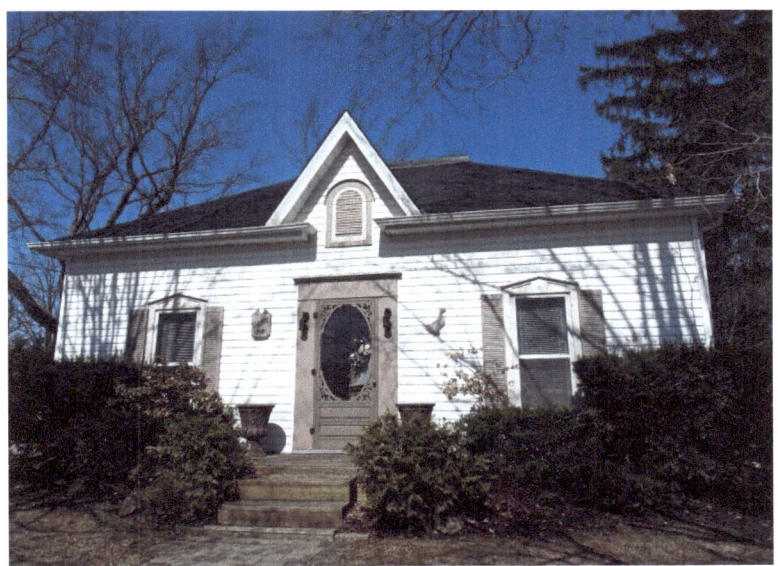

108 Mill Street – Gothic Revival cottage c. 1855

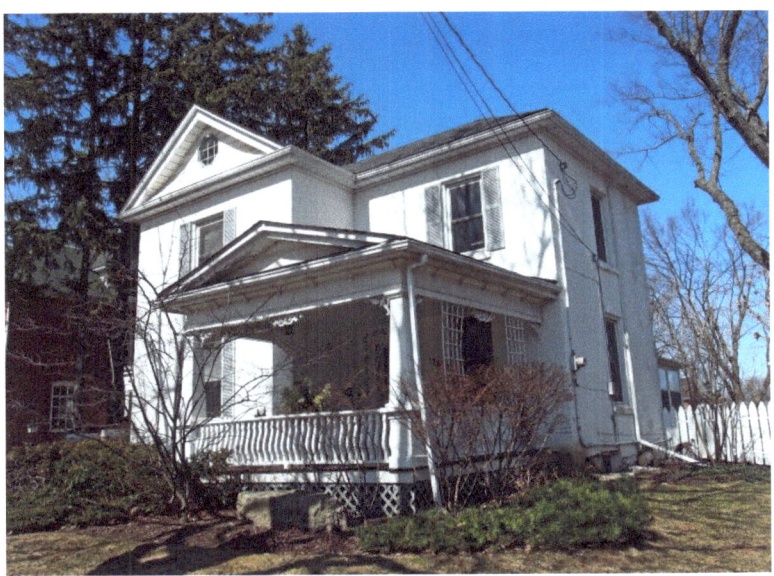

116 Mill Street – Italianate – pediment above verandah

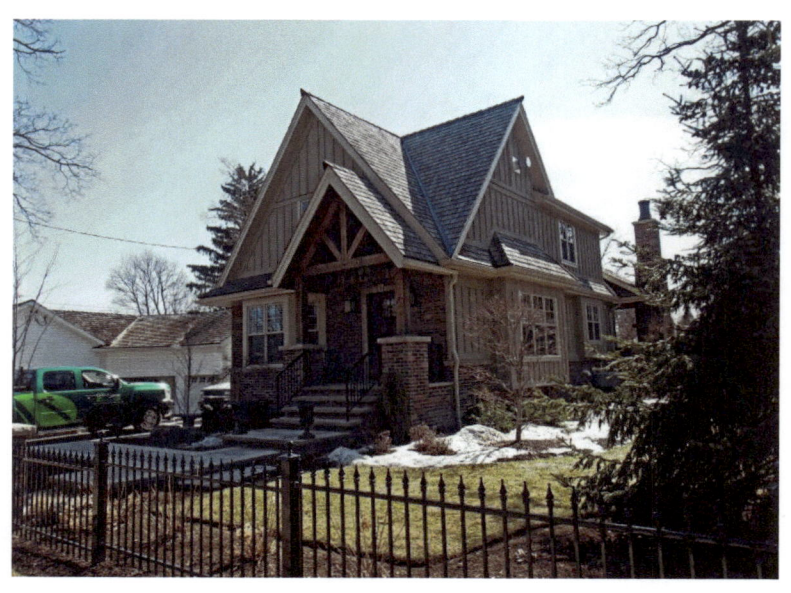

115 Mill Street – old Waterdown cottage

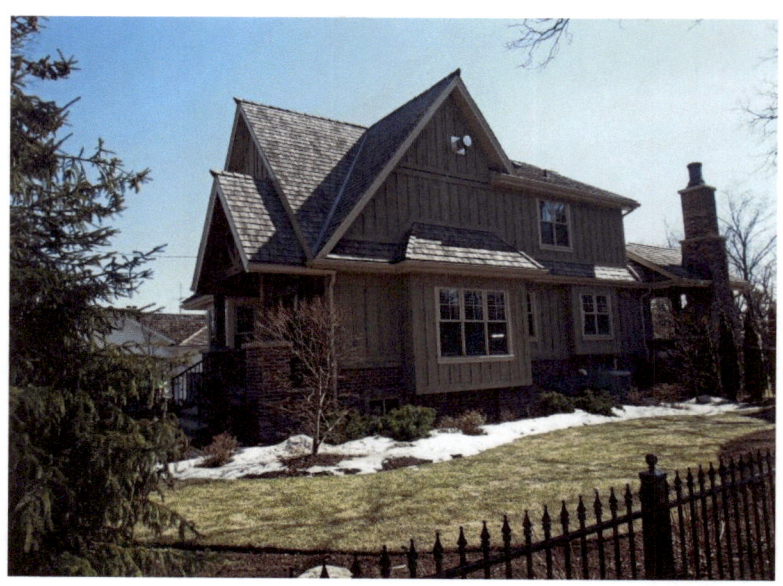

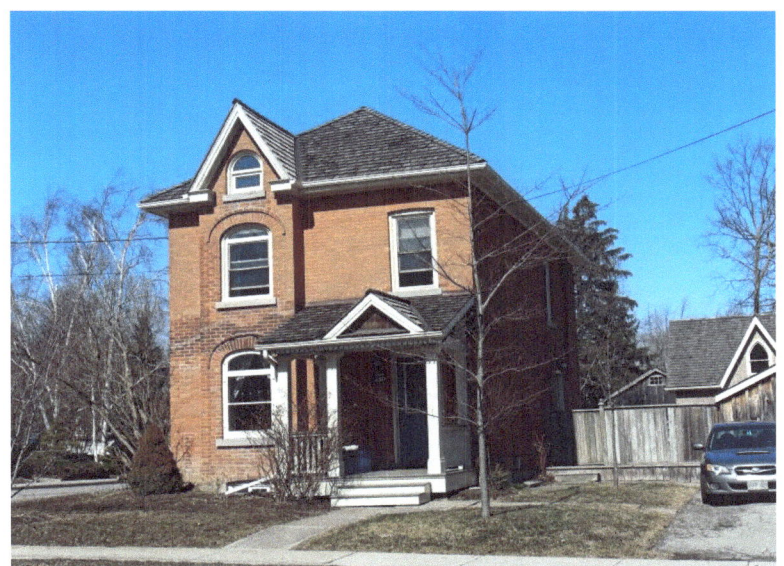

130 Mill Street – Italianate with two-and-a-half storey tower-like bay with cornice return on gable

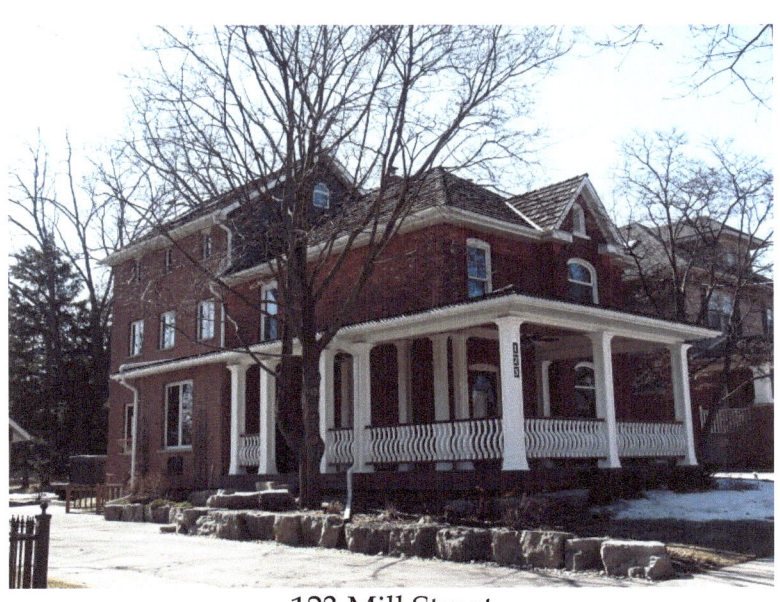

123 Mill Street

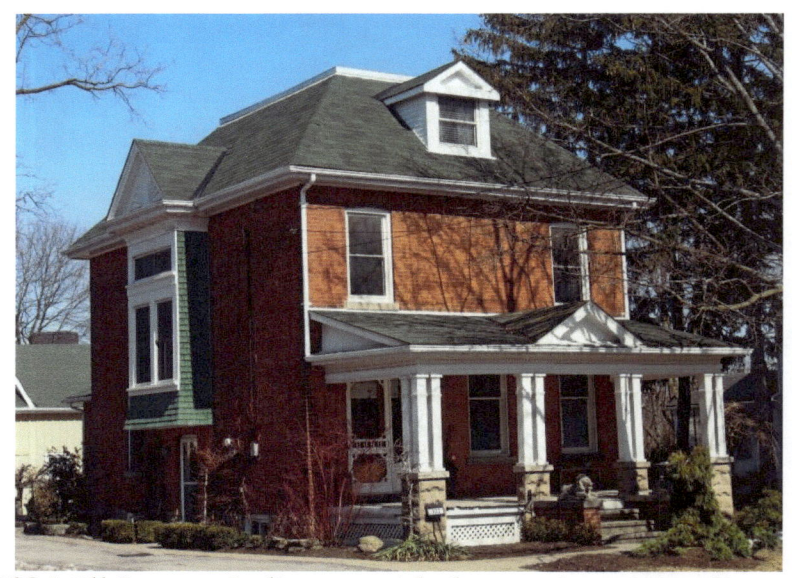

122 Mill Street – Italianate with dormer in attic, pediment above verandah

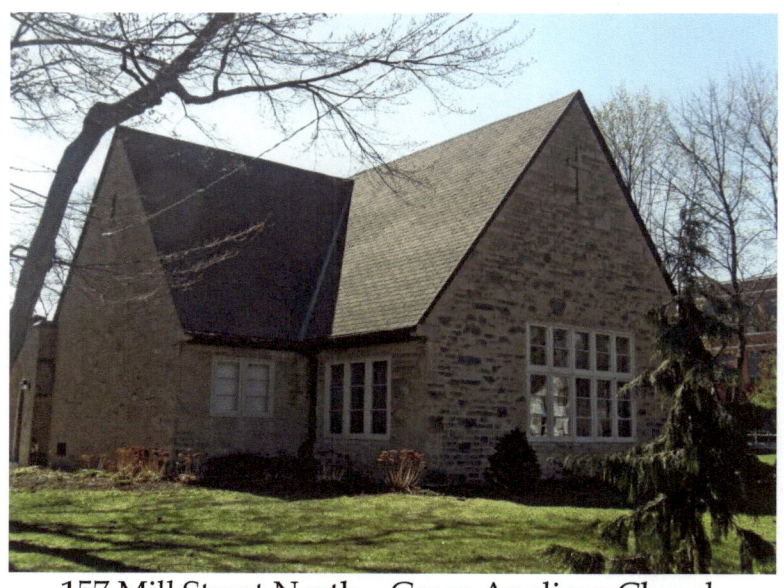

157 Mill Street North – Grace Anglican Church

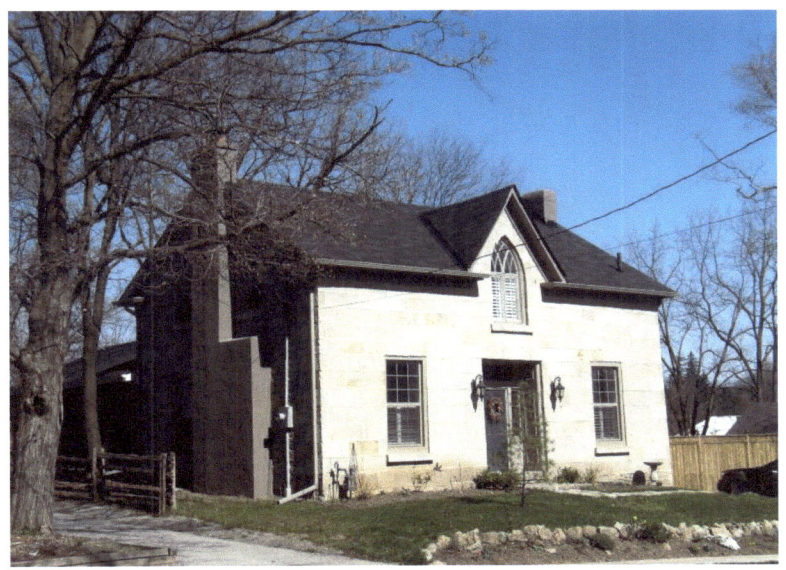

One-and-a-half storey Gothic Revival cottage

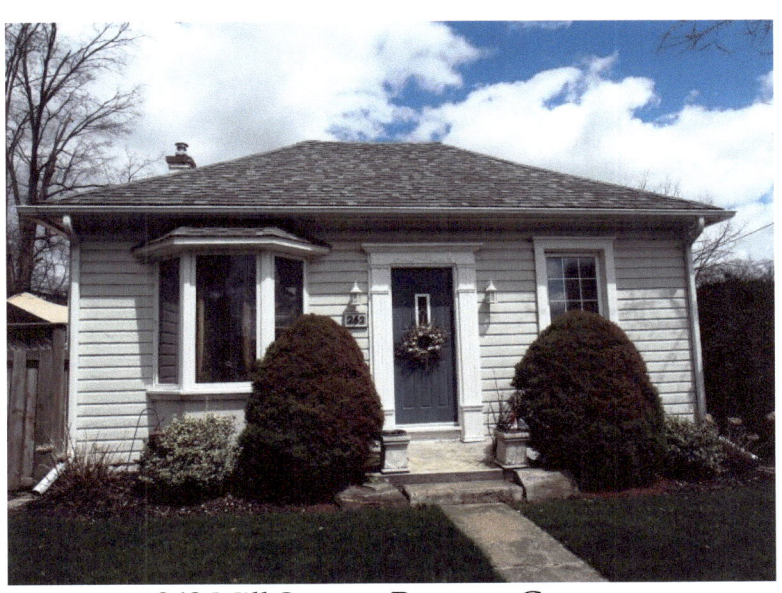

262 Mill Street – Regency Cottage

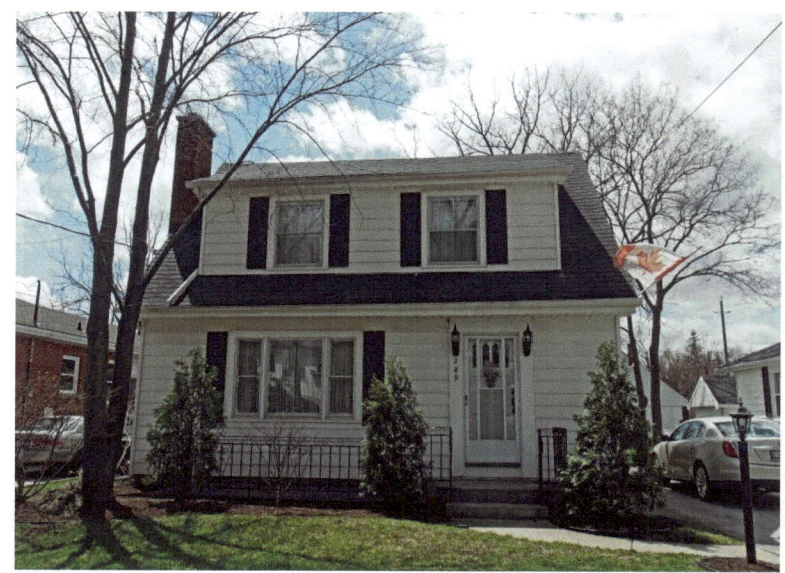

289 Mill Street

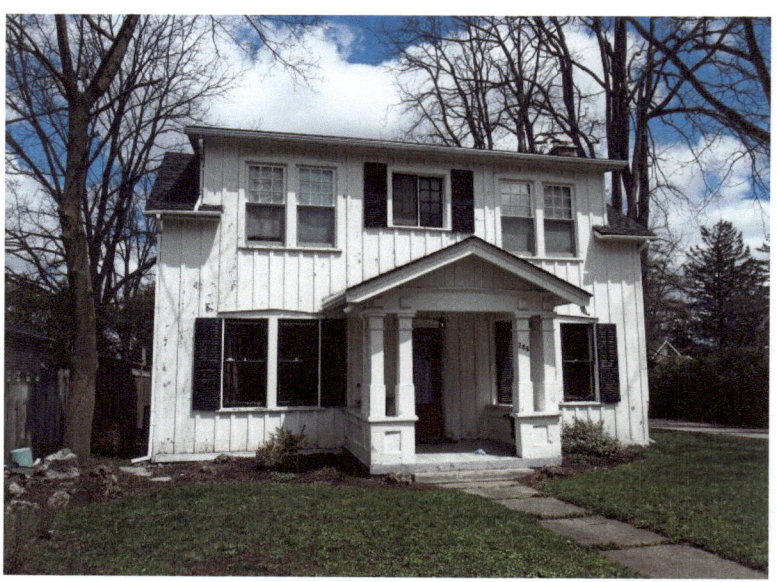

286 Mill Street - Georgian

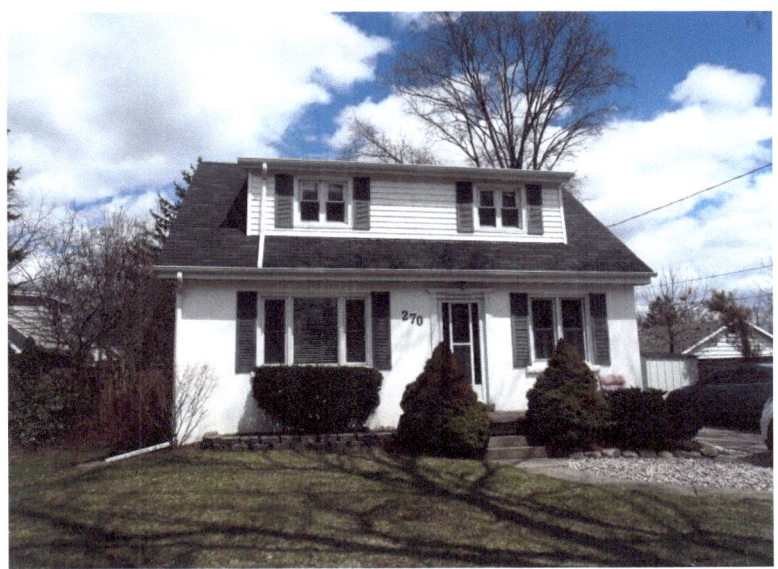

270 Mill Street

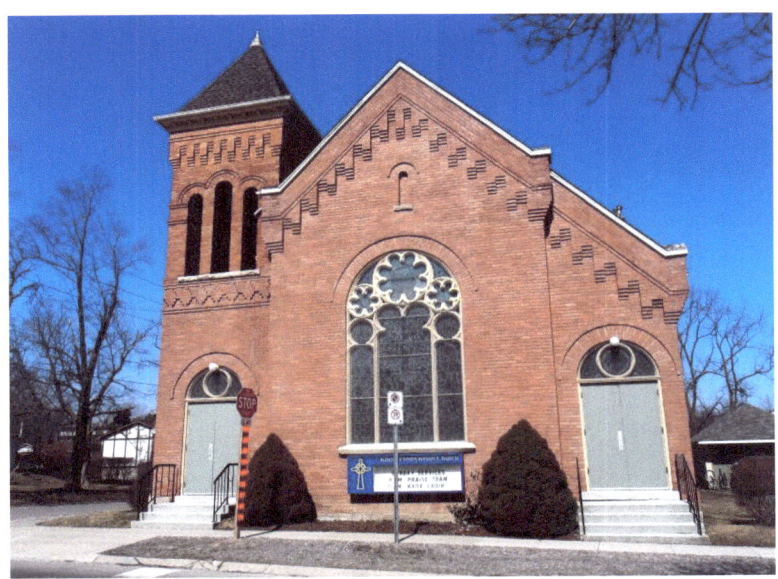

80 Mill Street North – Knox Presbyterian Church

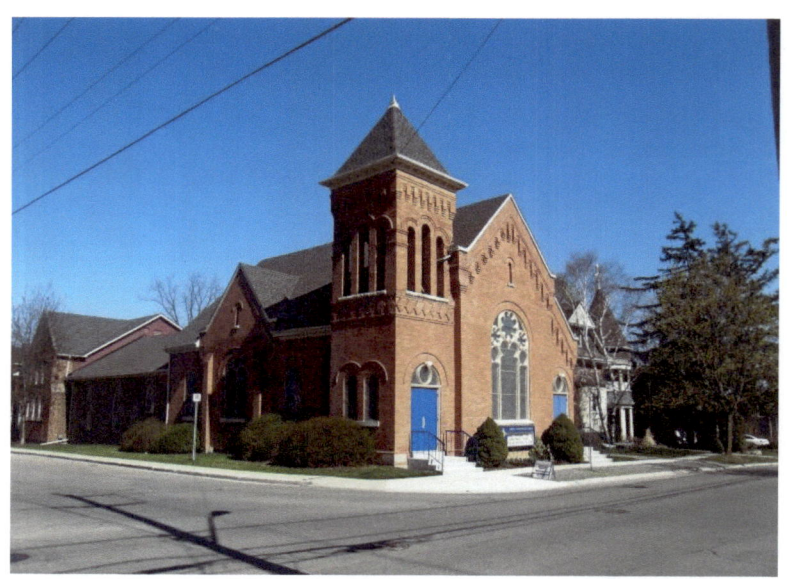

Bell tower, rose window, decorative brickwork

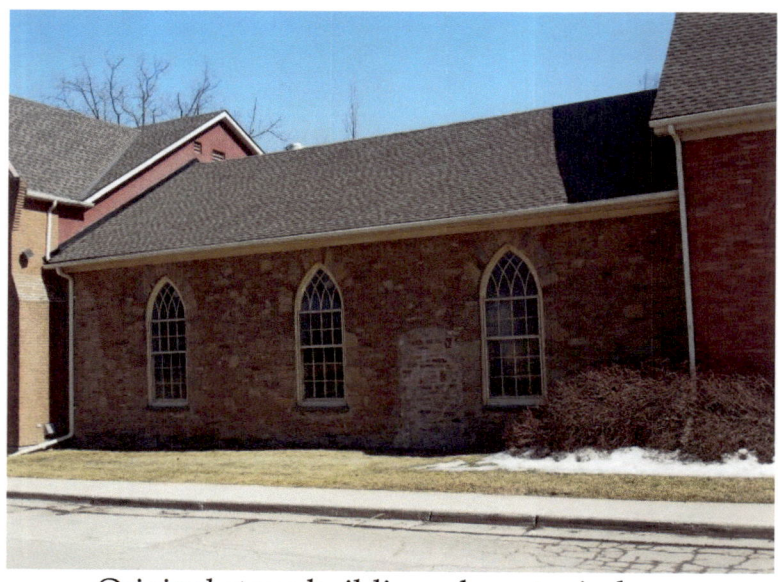

Original stone building – lancet windows

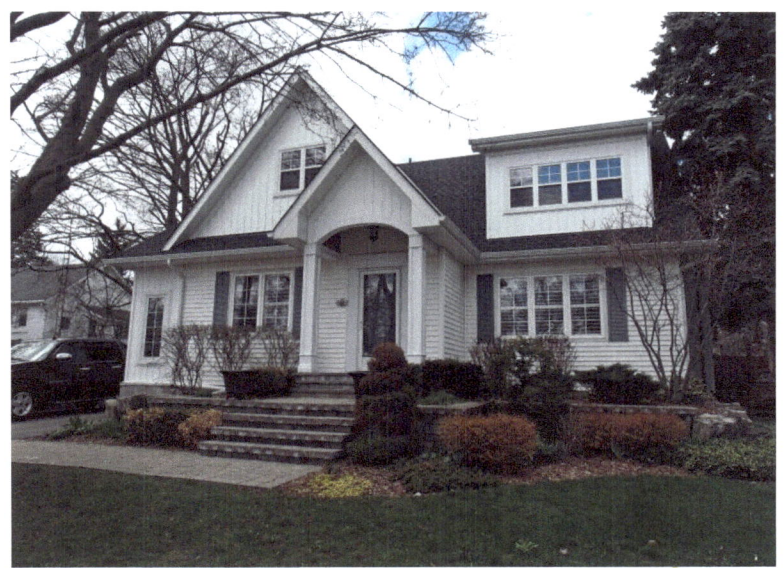

11 Church Street

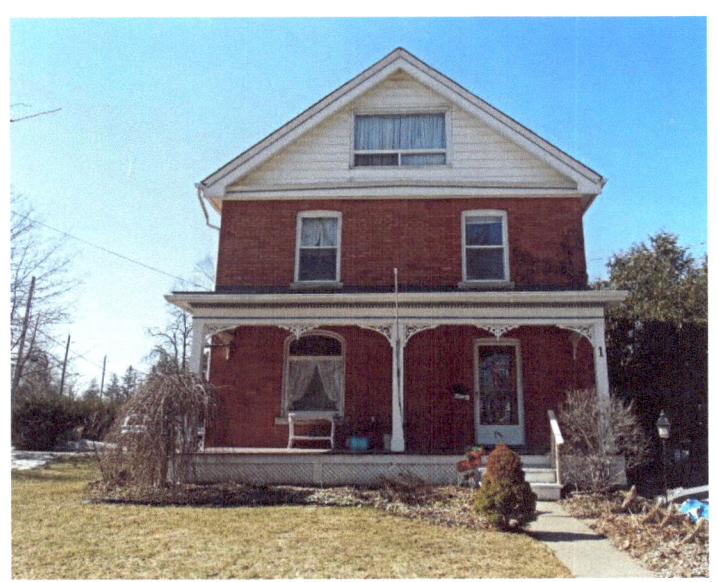

1 John Street – Edwardian

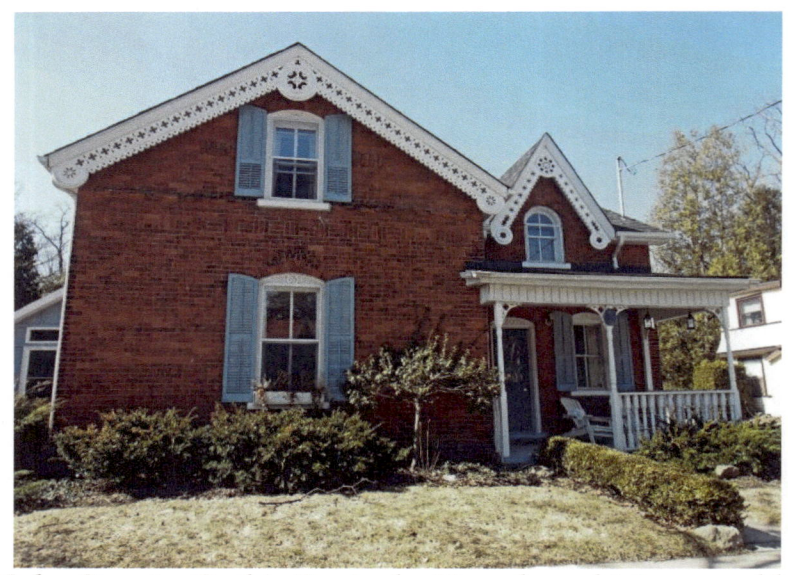

7 John Street – Gothic Revival – Vergeboard trim on gables

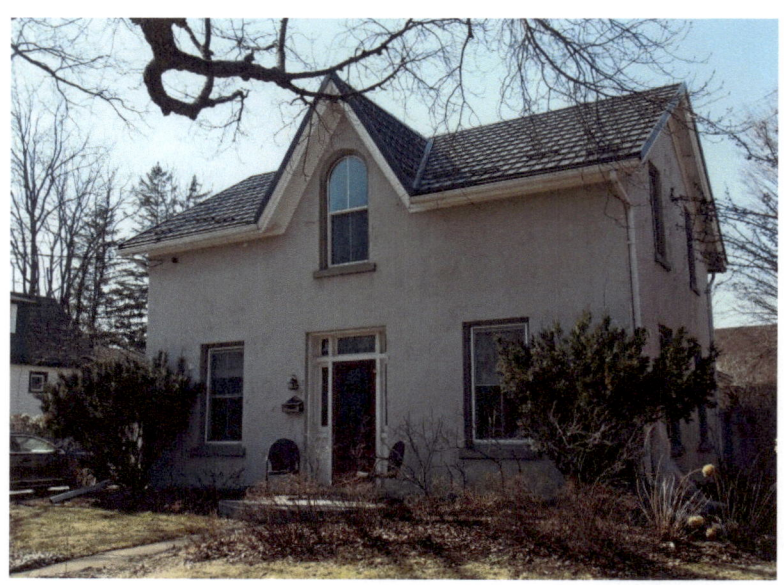

One-and-a-half storey Gothic Revival cottage

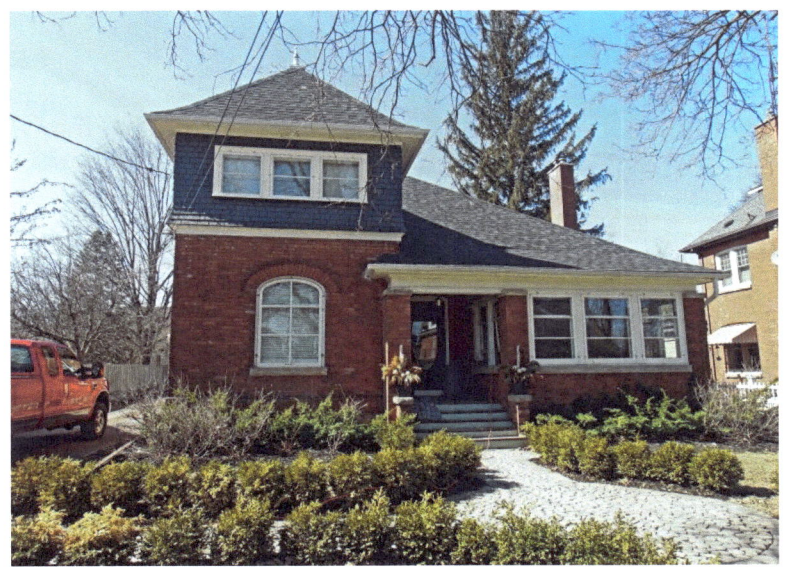

39 John Street

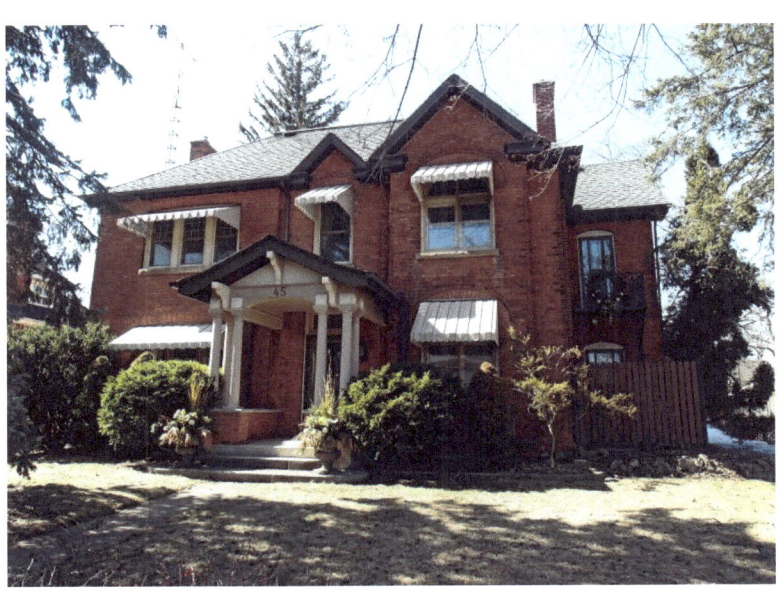

45 John Street

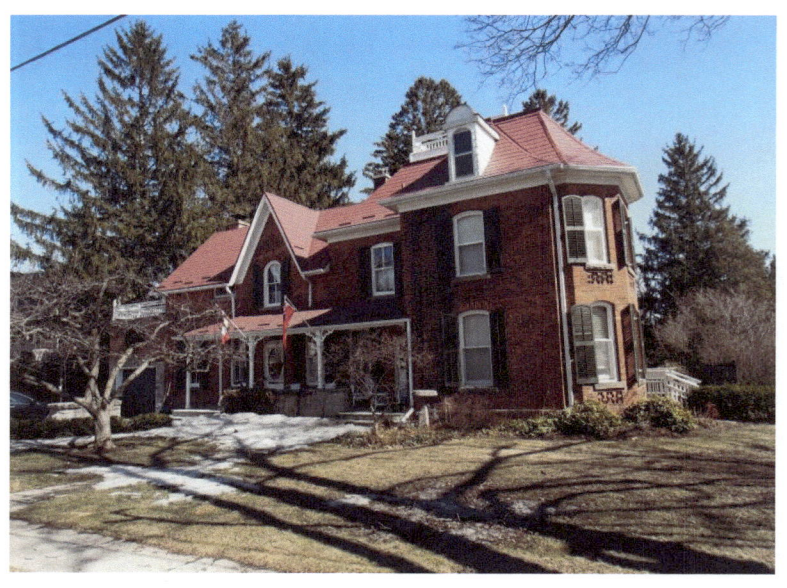

142 Main Street – Queen Anne style – balcony on rooftop, dormer windows, two-storey bays with tent roof

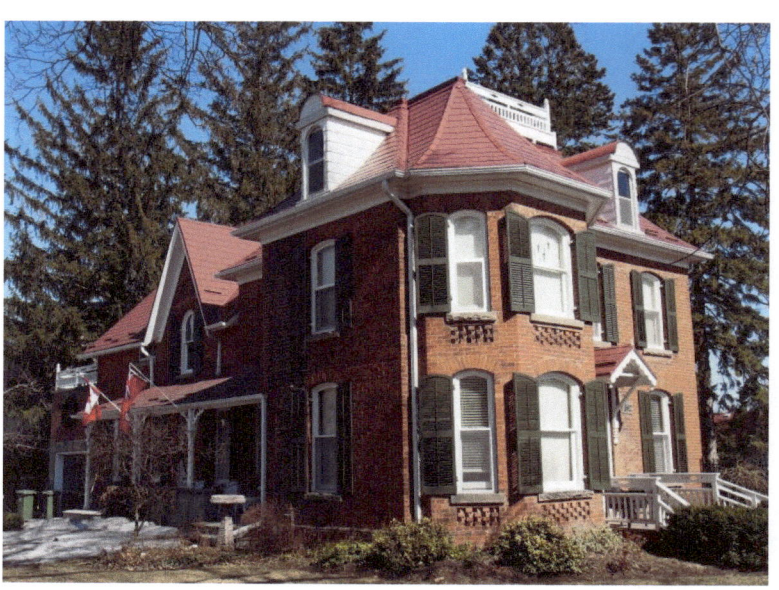

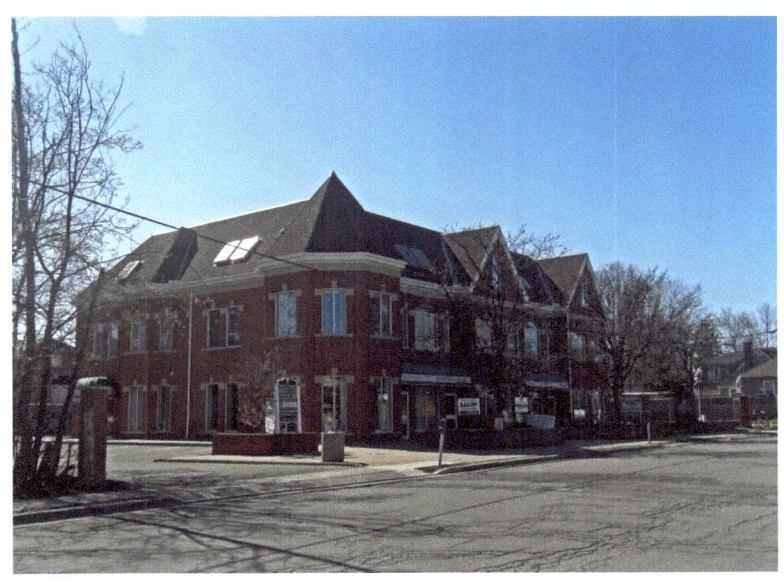

35 Main Street – two-storey tower with cone-shaped roof

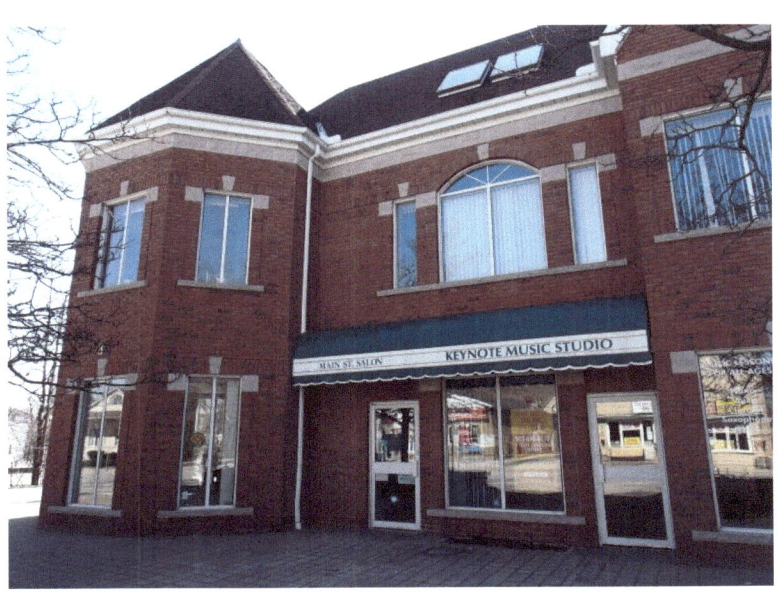

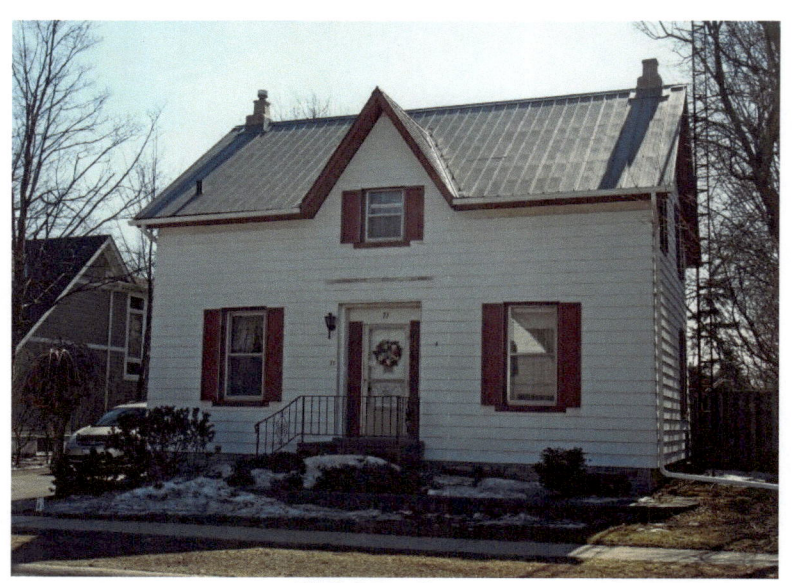

71 Main Street

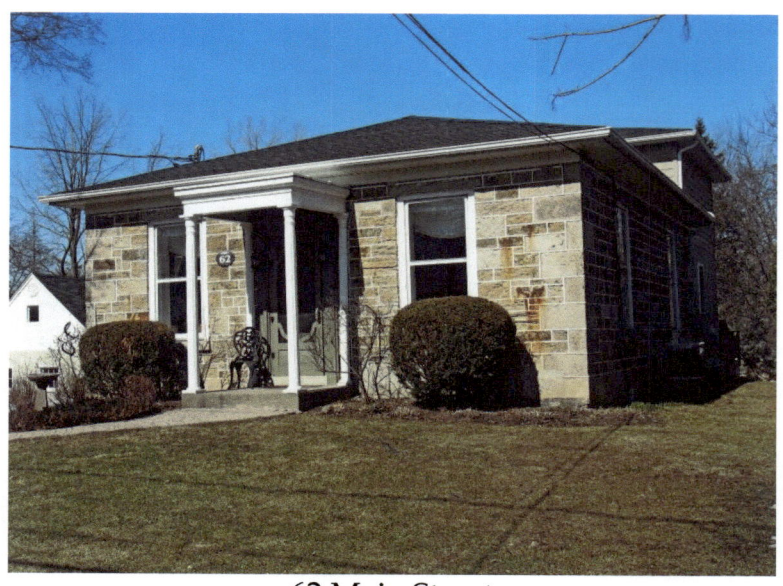

62 Main Street

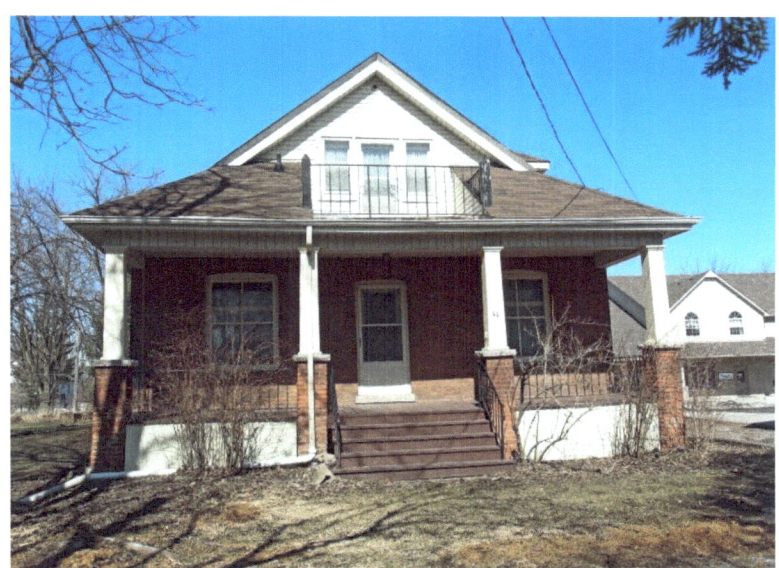

44 Main Street

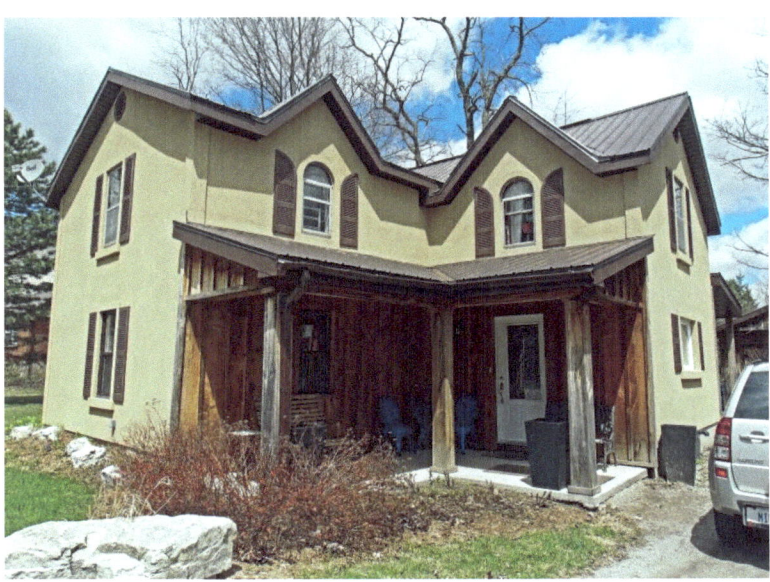

Main Street – Gothic Revival

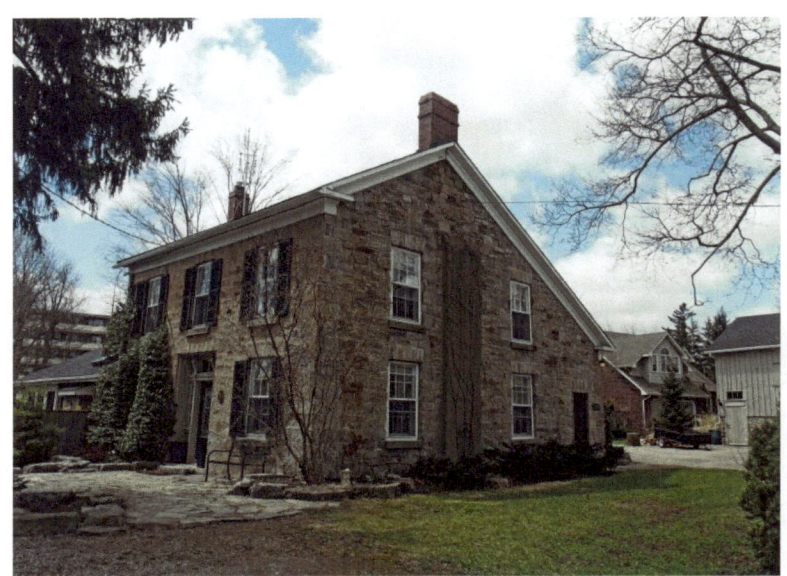

173 Main Street North – The Wallace House – c. 1840-1850 – cobblestone architecture, Georgian with Neo-Classical features, salt box shape (see appendix for description)

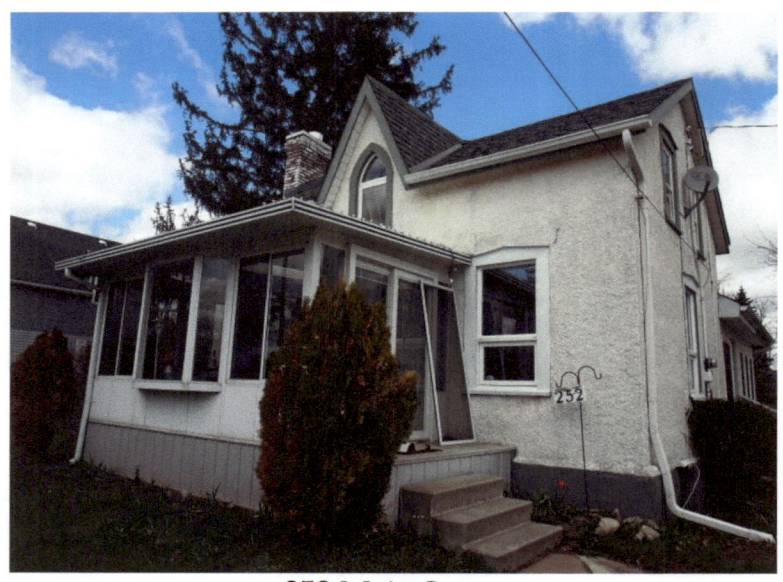

252 Main Street

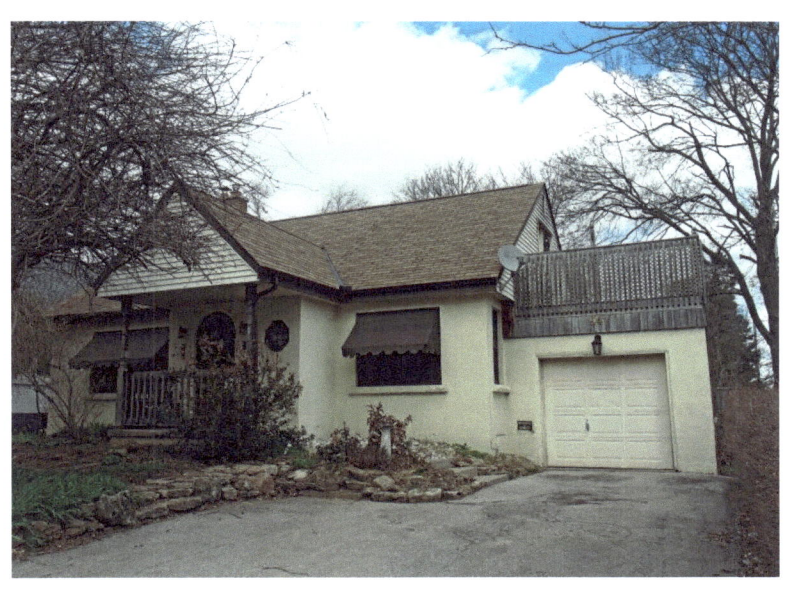

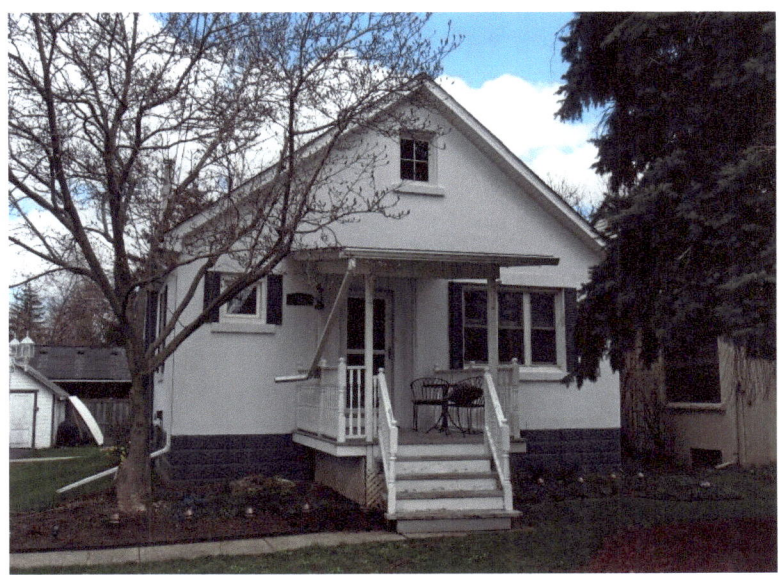

98 Main Street – Gothic Revival

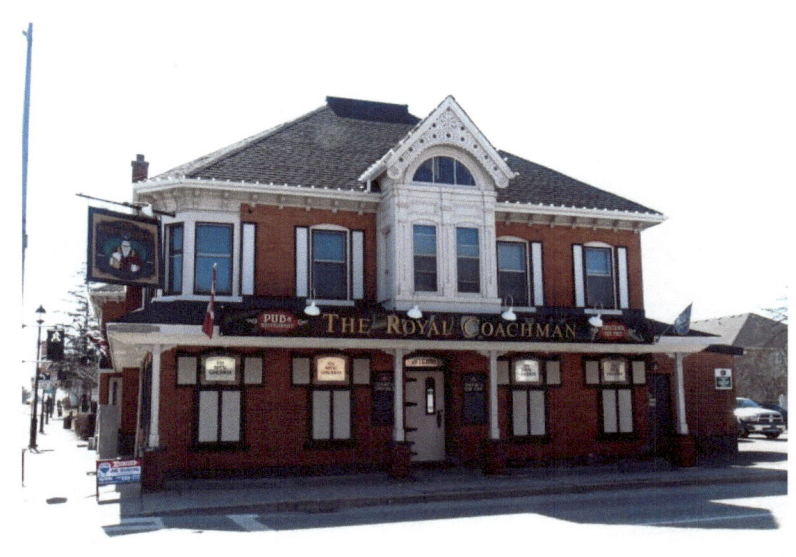

1 Main Street North – The Royal Coachman
– Victorian A.D. 1868

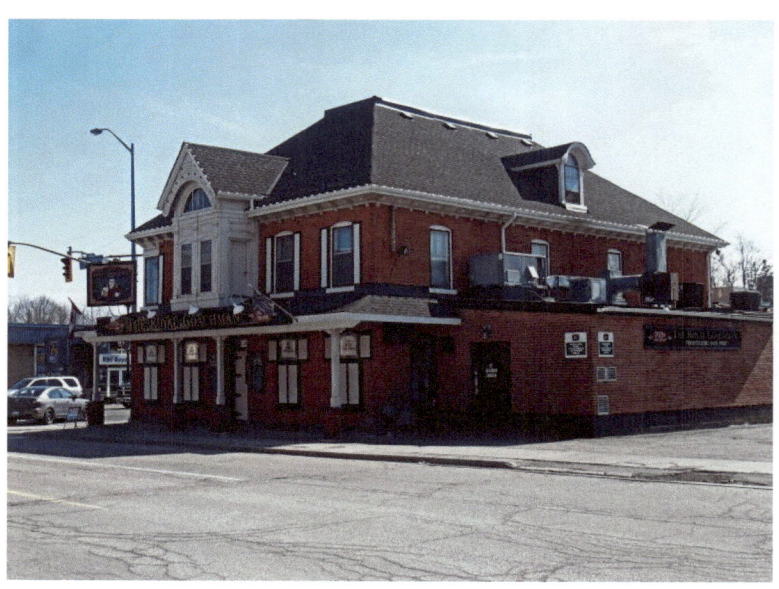

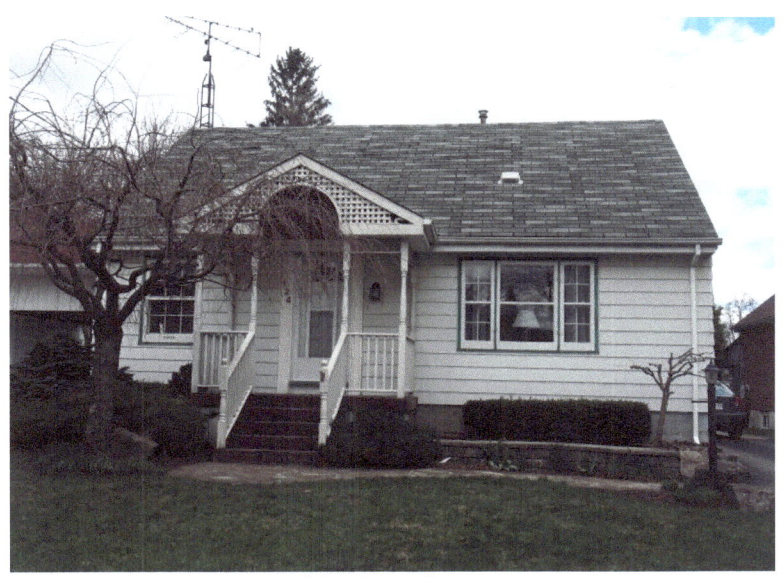

124 Main Street

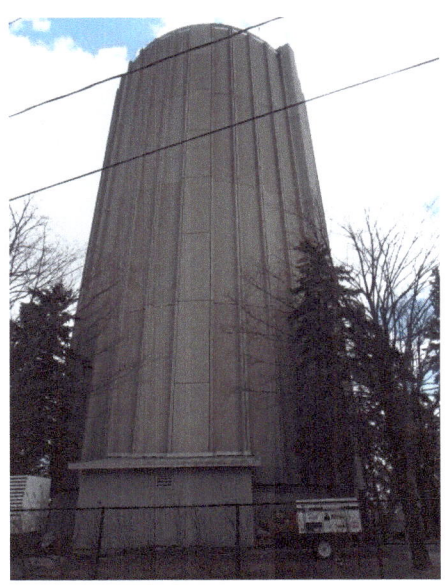

Kelly Street - Waterdown Water Works

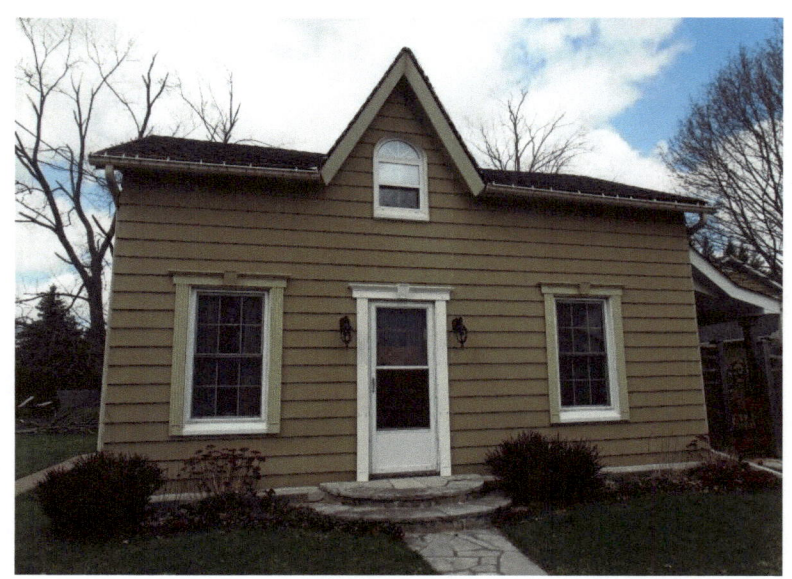

Kelly Street – Gothic Cottage

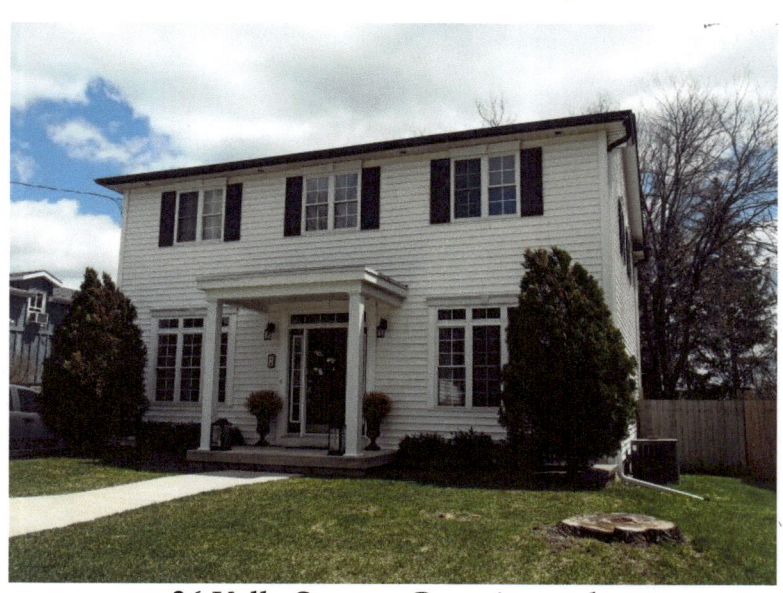

36 Kelly Street – Georgian style

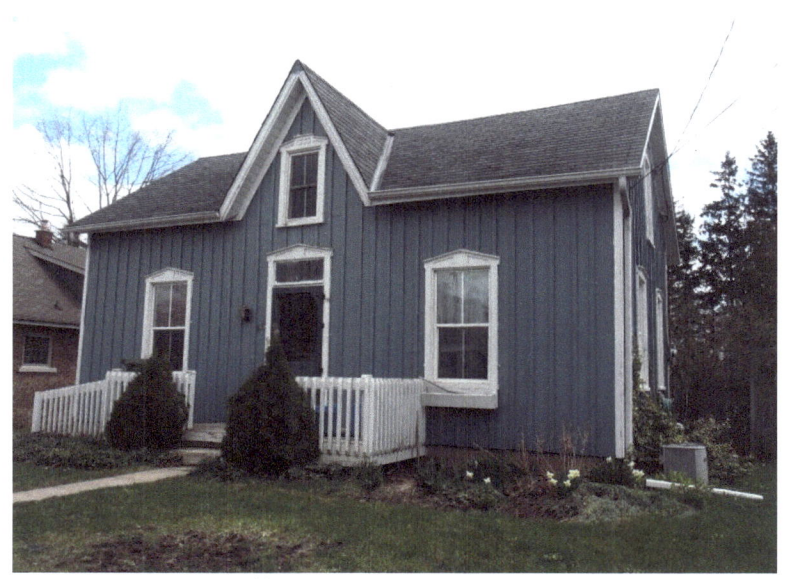

40 Kelly Street – Gothic Cottage

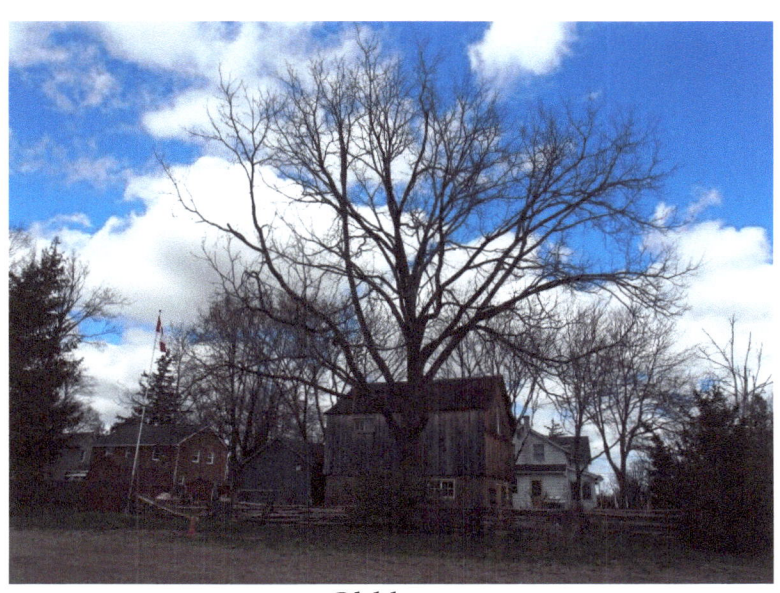

Old barn

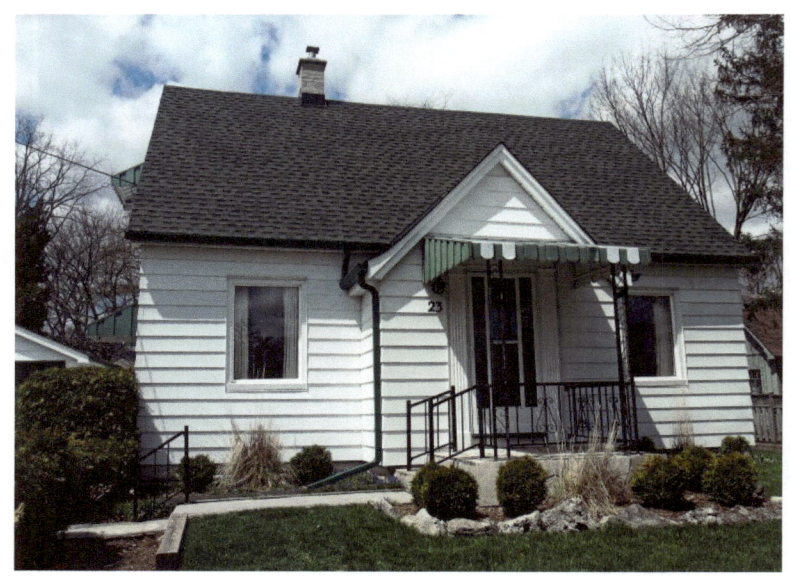

23 Wellington Street

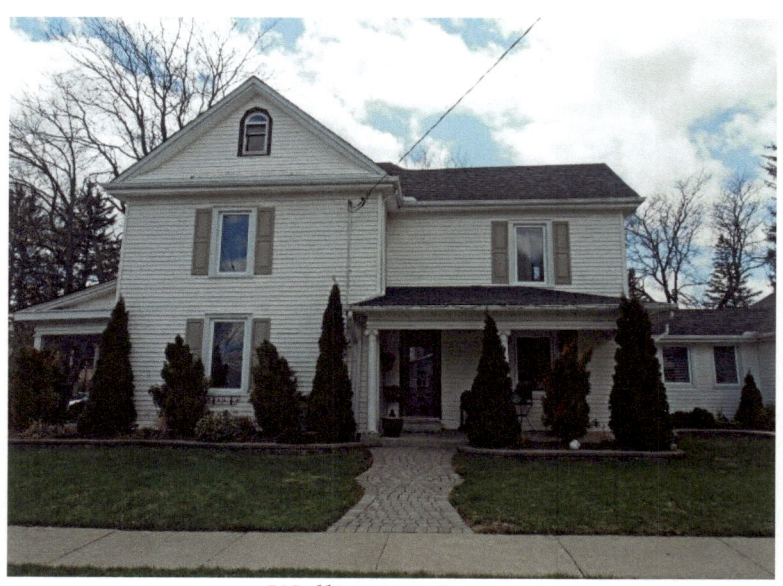

Wellington Street

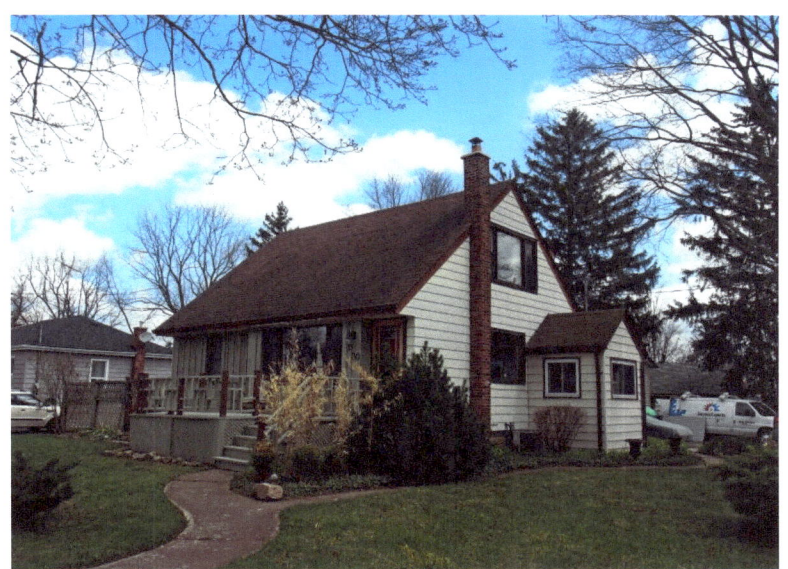

30 Wellington Street

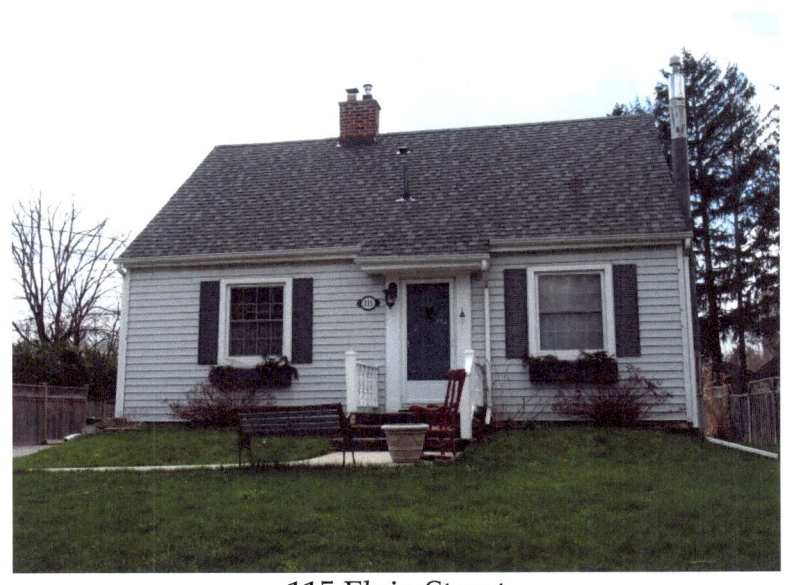

115 Elgin Street

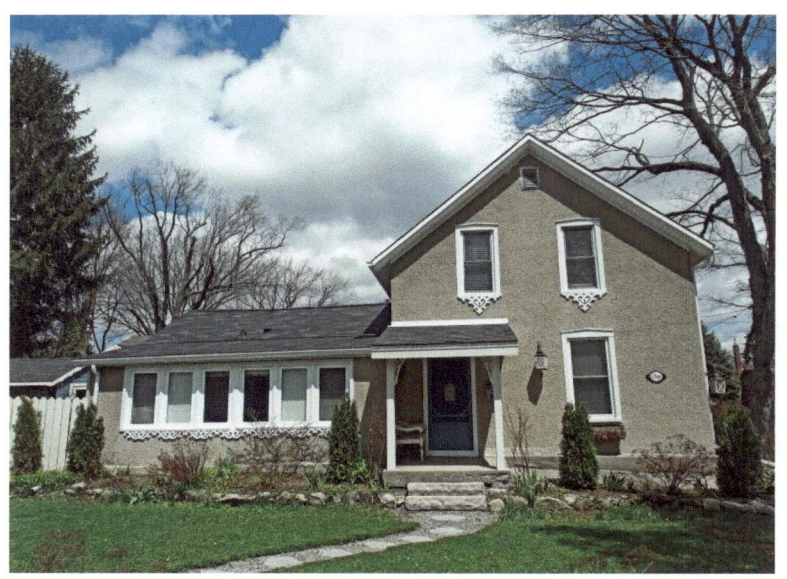

1 Elgin Street – Gothic Revival

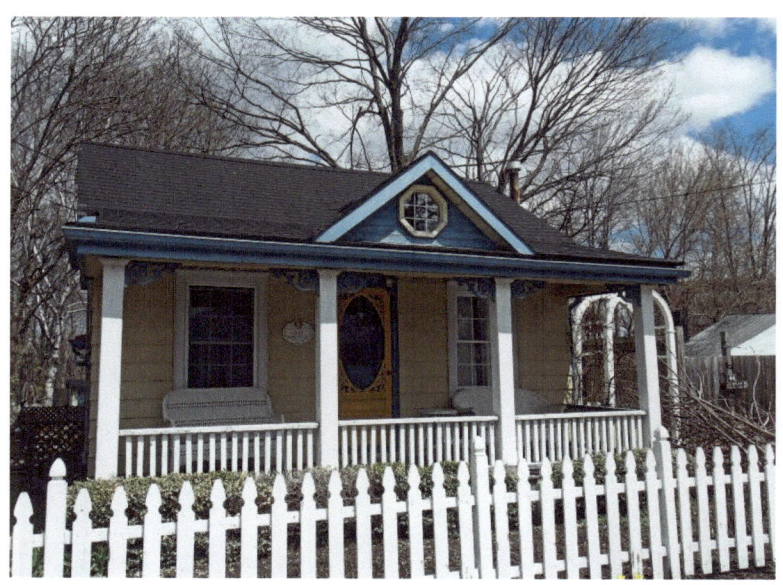

50 Elgin Street – Regency Cottage

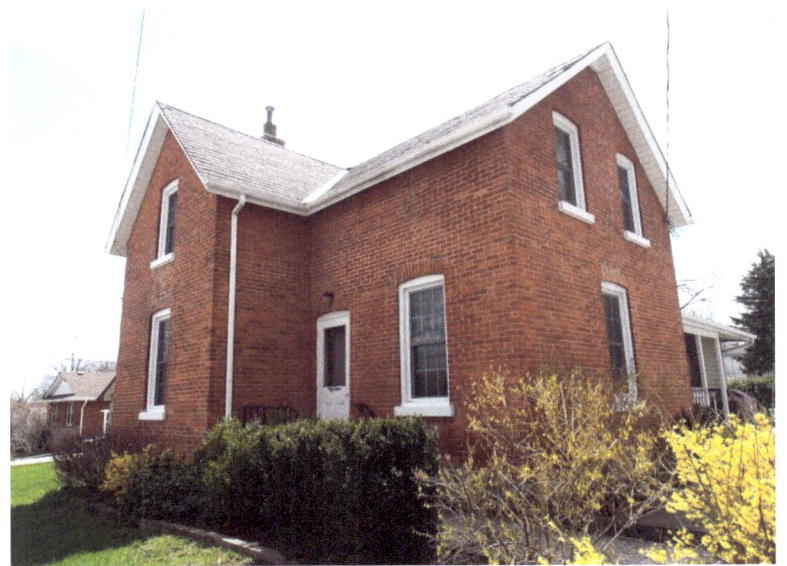

Elgin Street – Gothic Revival

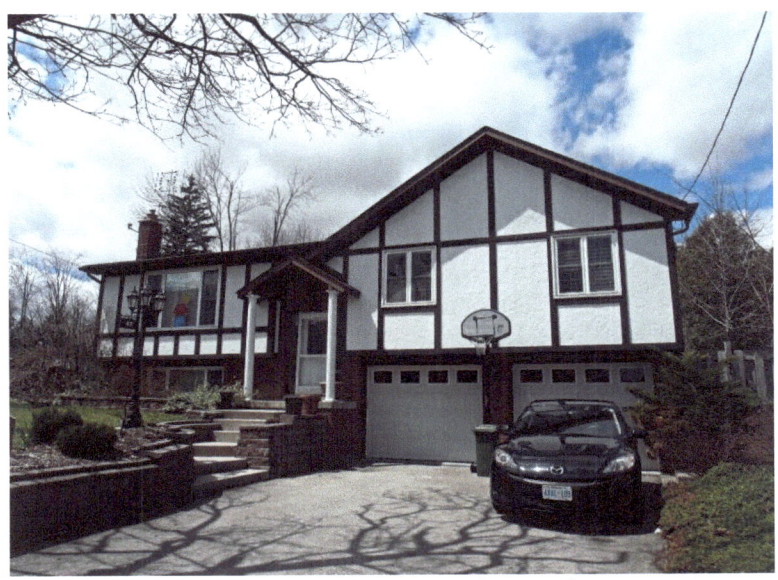

47 Elgin Street – Tudor style

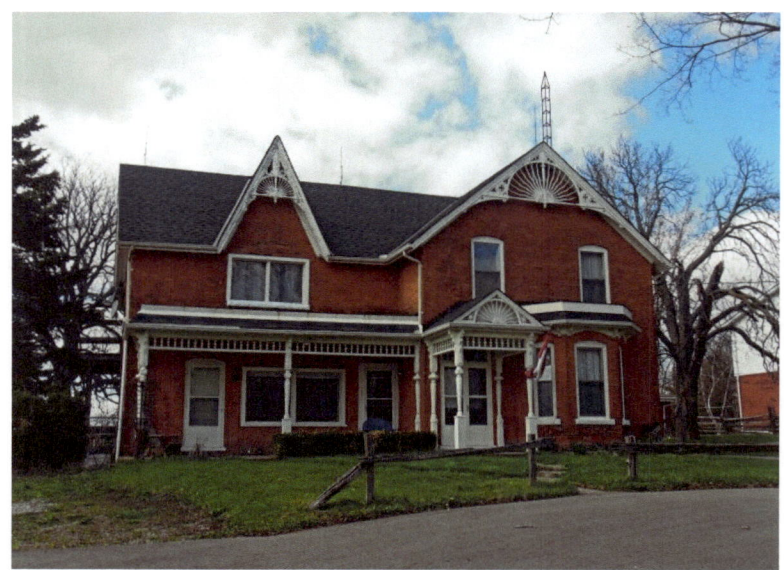

419 Parkside Drive – Gothic Revival – Vergeboard trim

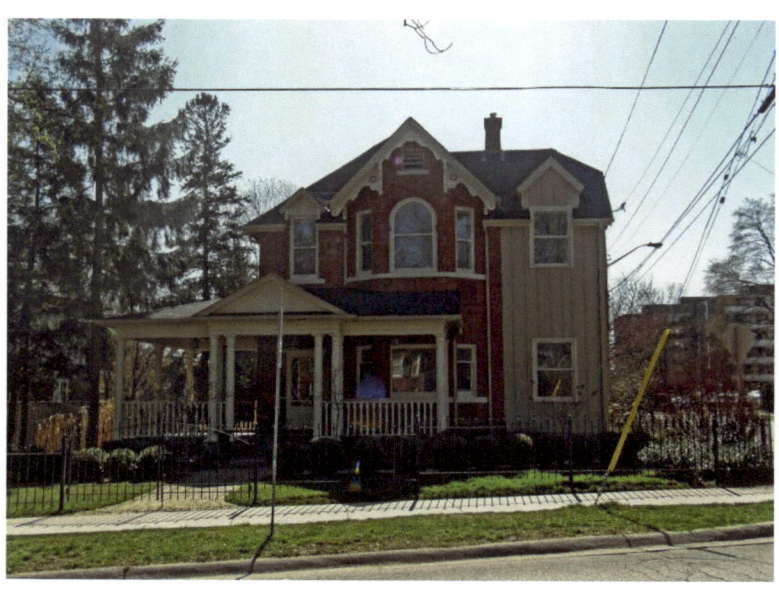

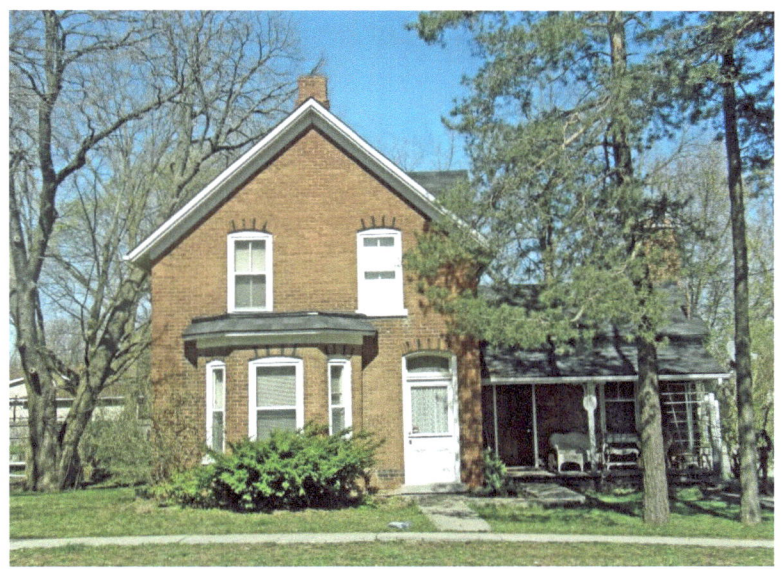

Gothic Revival – bay window on ground floor

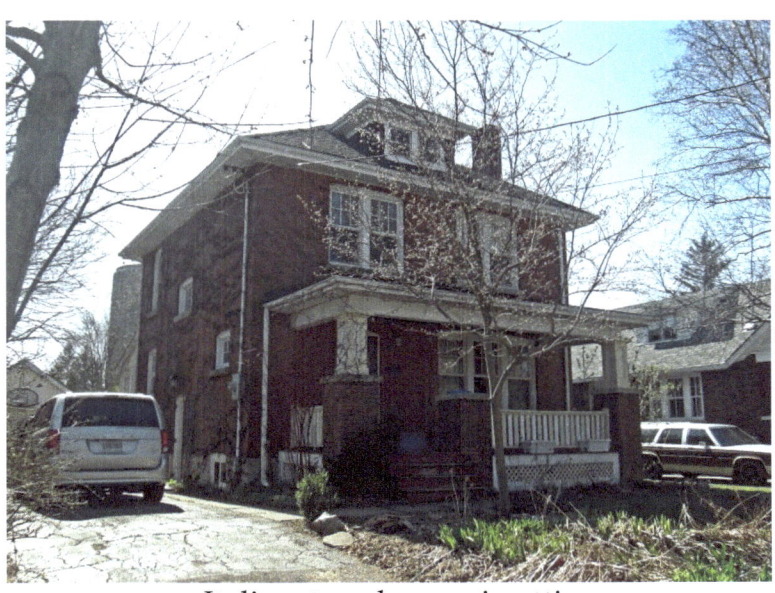

Italianate – dormer in attic

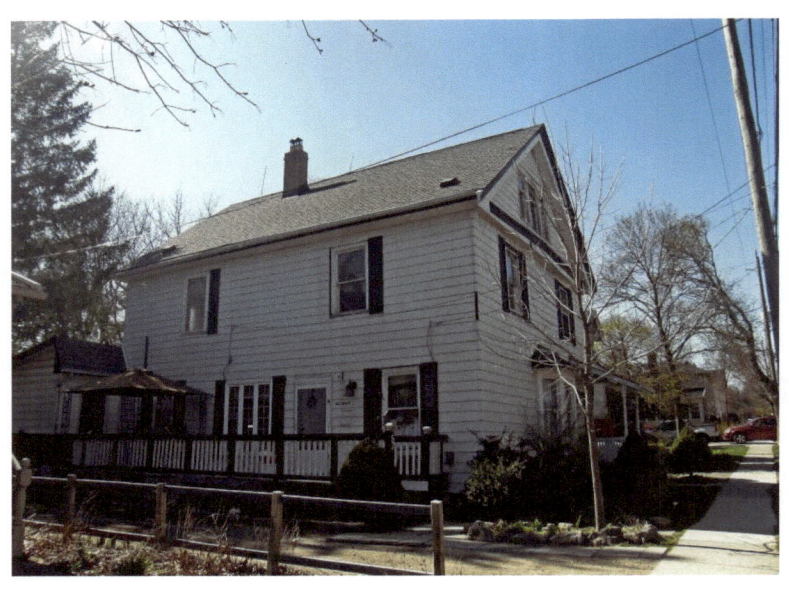

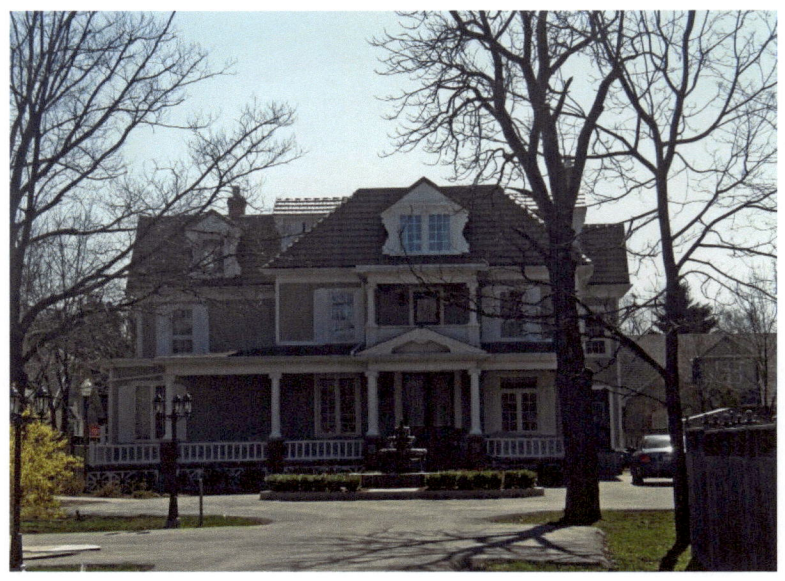

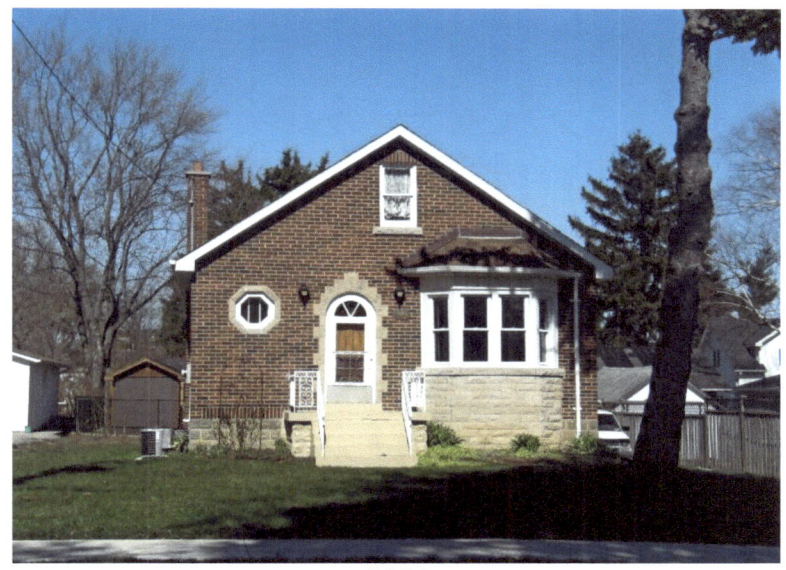

#104

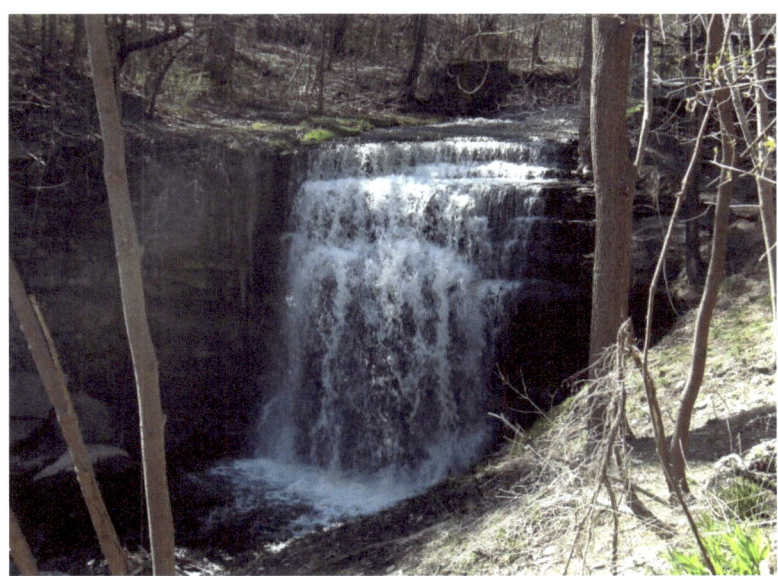

Grindstone Creek Waterfall

Rock Chapel Road

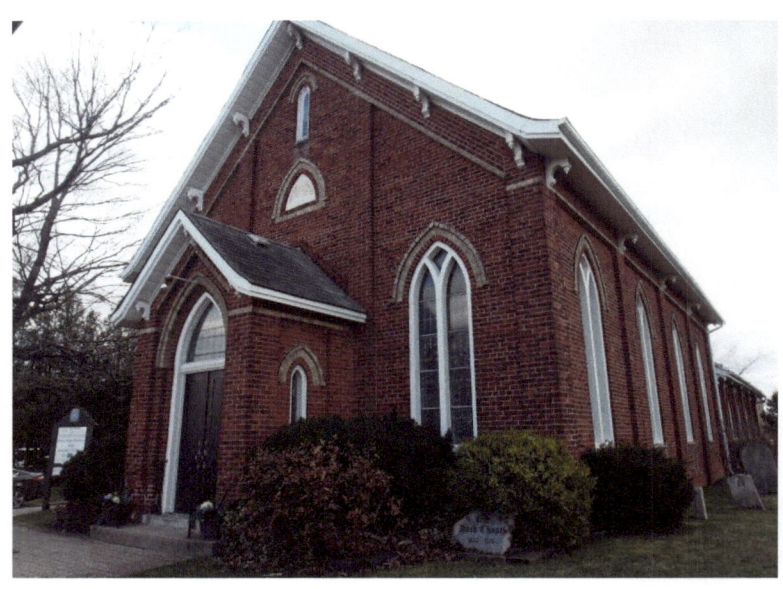

Rock Chapel United Church (old 1822-1876)

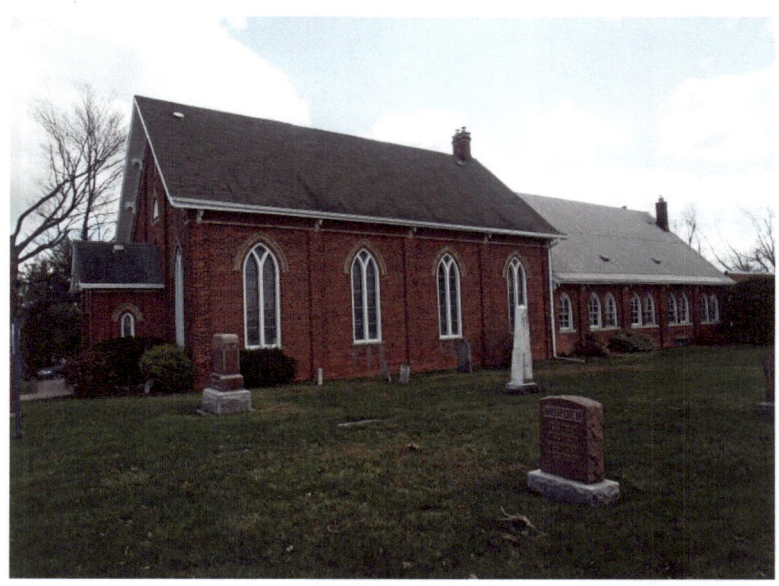

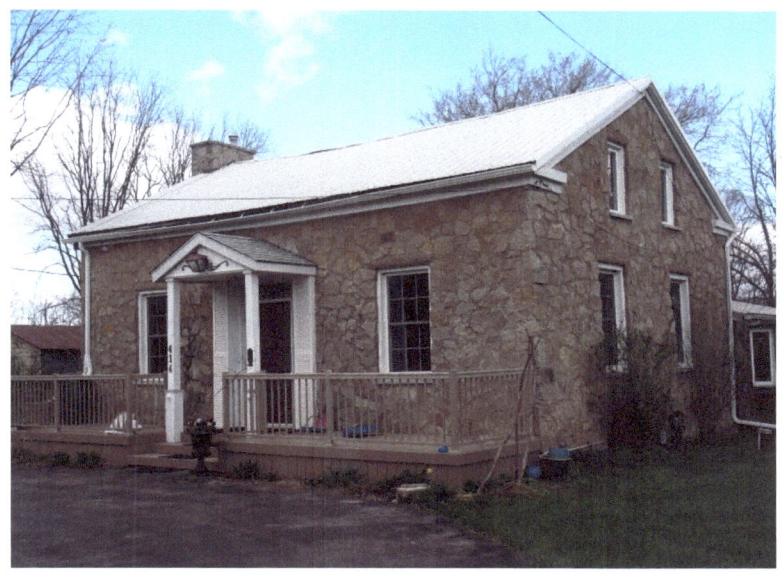

Rock Chapel Road – Gothic – cornice return on gable – cobblestone architecture

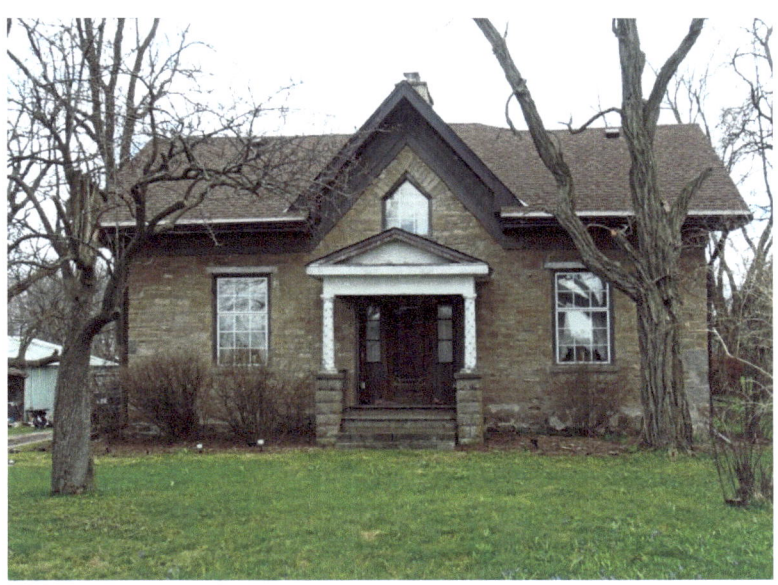

Rock Chapel Road – c. 1836 – frame house – stone added later

Architectural Terms

Brackets: a decorative or weight-bearing structural element which forms a right angle with one side against a wall and the other under a projecting surface such as an eave or roof. Example: 299 Dundas Street	
Capitals (Ionic): The uppermost finish or decoration on a column. Example: 94 Mill Street	
Cobblestone architecture: Refers to the use of cobblestones embedded in mortar as a method for erecting walls on houses and commercial buildings. Example: 134 Mill Street	
Cornice: originally the wooden overhang of the roof. With the use of stone, brick, iron and steel, the cornice is any projecting shelf at the top of a ceiling or roof. They can be very decorative. Example: 299 Dundas Street	
Cornice Return: decorative element on the end of a gable. Example: Rock Chapel Road	
Dentil Moulding: an even series of rectangles used as ornamental decoration in cornices. Example: Waterdown Memorial Hall	
Entablature: On Classical buildings, the entire horizontal mass carried above the columns. Entablatures usually contain an architrave, a frieze, and a cornice. Example: Dundas Street – Memorial Hall	

Dormer: (French for "sleep") a gable end window that pierces through the plane of a sloping roof surface to create usable space in the top floor or attic of a building by adding headroom. Example: 302 Dundas Street	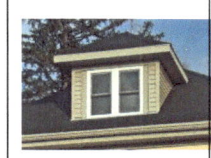
Finial: ornament added to the top of a gable, pinnacle, canopy or spire – a Gothic element. Example: 76 Mill Street	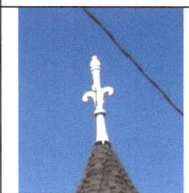
Gable: the triangular portion of a wall between the edges of a sloping roof. Example: 289 Dundas Street	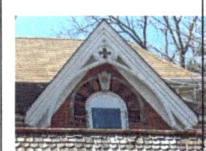
Hipped Roof: a roof where all sides slope downwards to the walls with no gables. Example: 122 Mill Street	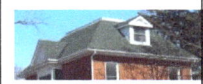
Keystones and Voussoirs: a voussoir is a wedge-shaped element used in building an arch. A keystone is the central stone that locks all the stones into position, allowing the arch to bear weight. A keystone is often enlarged and embellished. Example: 299 Dundas Street and Memorial Hall	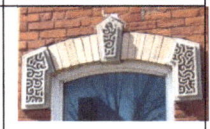 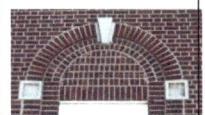
Lancet Window: a tall, narrow window with a pointed arch at its top. Example: 80 Mill Street North	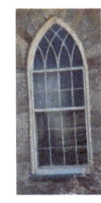

Mansard Roof: This style was popularized by Francois Mansart (1598-1666), an accomplished architect of the French Baroque period and especially fashionable during the Second French Empire (1852-1870). This roof is almost flat on the top section, with two slopes on each of its sides with the lower slope at a steeper angle than the upper and having dormer windows. Example: 299 Dundas Street	
Pediment: a triangular section above the horizontal structure (entablature), typically supported by columns. The inside of the triangle is called the tympanum. Example: 94 Mill Street	
Rose Window: a circular window with ornamental tracery radiating from the centre. Example: 80 Mill Street North	
Salt Box: is a building with a long pitched roof that slopes down to the back – one storey in the back and two storeys in the front. Example: 173 Main Street North	
Turret: a small tower that projects from the wall of a building. Example: 76 Mill Street	
Vergeboards: also called bargeboards – hang from the projecting end of a roof and are often elaborately carved and ornamented. Example: 50 Mill Street	

Waterdown's Building Styles

Edwardian, 1900-1930 – This style bridges the ornate and elaborate styles of the Victorian era and the simplified styles of the 20th century. Balanced facades, simple roof lines, dormer windows, large front porches, and smooth brick surfaces are its characteristics. Example: 1 John Street	
Georgian, before 1860 – This style began with the British King Georges in the 18th century. These buildings have balanced facades around a central door, medium-pitched gable roofs, and small paned windows. Example: 36 Kelly Street	
Gothic Revival, 1830-1890 – These decorative buildings have sharply-pitched gables with highly detailed vergeboards, pointed-arch window openings, and dichromatic brickwork. It is a common style in Ontario. Examples: 315 Dundas Street	
Italianate, 1850-1900 – It has wide-bracketed eaves, belvederes, wrap-around verandahs. Examples: 122 Mill Street	
Queen Anne, 1885-1900 – This style is distinguished by an irregular outline featuring a combination of an offset tower, broad gables, projecting two-storey bays, verandahs, multi-sloped roofs, and tall, decorative chimneys. A mixture of brick and wood is common. Windows often have one large single-paned bottom sash and small panes in the upper sash. Example: 289 Dundas Street	

Regency Cottage, 1830-1860 – This style originated in England in 1815 and spread to Ontario later in the 19th century as British officers retired to Canada. It is a modest one-storey house with a low-pitched hip roof and has a symmetrical front façade. Example: 43 Mill Street	
Romanesque Revival, 1880-1910 – This style hearkens back to medieval architecture of the 11th and 12th centuries with a heavy appearance, blocky towers and rounded arches. Example of Romanesque style window hood: Mill Street	
Second Empire, 1860-1880 – The mansard roof is the most noteworthy feature of this style and is evidence of the French origins. Projecting central towers and one or two-storey bays can also be present. Example: 299 Dundas Street	
Tudor Revival – exposed timbers with stucco infill, multi-paned windows. Example: 47 Elgin Street	

www.ingramcontent.com/pod-product-compliance
Lightning Source LLC
Chambersburg PA
CBHW040841180526
45159CB00001B/266